The Vietnam War

The Vietnam War examines this conflict from its origins up until North Vietnam's victory in 1975. Historian Mitchell K. Hall's lucid account is an ideal introduction to the key debates surrounding a war that remains controversial and disputed in American scholarship and collective memory.

The new edition has been fully updated and expanded to include additional material on the preceding French–Indochina War, the American antiwar movement, North Vietnamese perspectives and motivations, and the postwar scholarly debate. The text is supported by a documents section and a wide range of study tools, including a timeline of events, glossaries of key figures and terms, and a rich "further reading" section accompanied by a new bibliographical essay. Concise yet comprehensive, *The Vietnam War* remains the most accessible and stimulating introduction to this crucial twentieth-century conflict.

Mitchell K. Hall is Professor of History at Central Michigan University. His most recent works include *The Vietnam War Era: People and Perspectives* (2009); *The Emergence of Rock and Roll: Music and the Rise of American Youth Culture* (2014); and *Opposition to War: An Encyclopedia of U.S. Peace and Antiwar Movements* (2018).

Introduction To The Series

History is the narrative constructed by historians from traces left by the past. Historical enquiry is often driven by contemporary issues and, in consequence, historical narratives are constantly reconsidered, reconstructed, and reshaped. The fact that different historians have different perspectives on issues means that there is often controversy and no universally agreed version of past events. *Seminar Studies* was designed to bridge the gap between current research and debate, and the broad, popular general surveys that often date rapidly.

The volumes in the series are written by historians who are not only familiar with the latest research and current debates concerning their topic, but who have themselves contributed to our understanding of the subject. The books are intended to provide the reader with a clear introduction to a major topic in history. They provide both a narrative of events and a critical analysis of contemporary interpretations. They include the kinds of tools generally omitted from specialist monographs: a chronology of events, a glossary of terms, and brief biographies of "who's who." They also include bibliographical essays in order to guide students to the literature on various aspects of the subject. Students and teachers alike will find that the selection of documents will stimulate the discussion and offer insight into the raw materials used by historians in their attempt to understand the past.

Clive Emsley and Gordon Martel
Series Editors

The Vietnam War

Third Edition

Mitchell K. Hall

Routledge
Taylor & Francis Group

NEW YORK AND LONDON

Third edition published 2018
by Routledge
711 Third Avenue, New York, NY 10017

and by Routledge
2 Park Square, Milton Park, Abingdon, Oxon, OX14 4RN

Routledge is an imprint of the Taylor & Francis Group, an informa business

First edition published by Pearson Education Ltd. 2000

Second edition published by Pearson Education Ltd. 2007

Library of Congress Cataloging-in-Publication Data
Names: Hall, Mitchell K., author.
Title: The Vietnam War / by Mitchell K. Hall.
Description: Third edition. | New York : Routledge, 2018. | Series: Seminar
    studies | Includes bibliographical references and index.
Identifiers: LCCN 2017045925 (print) | LCCN 2017046205 (ebook) |
    ISBN 9781315542874 | ISBN 9781138685994 (alk. paper)
Subjects: LCSH: Vietnam War, 1961–1975.
Classification: LCC DS557.7 (ebook) | LCC DS557.7 .H32 2018 (print) |
    DDC 959.704/3–dc23
LC record available at https://lccn.loc.gov/2017045925

ISBN: 978-1-138-68599-4 (hbk)
ISBN: 978-1-138-68600-7 (pbk)
ISBN: 978-1-315-54287-4 (ebk)

Typeset in Sabon
by Apex CoVantage, LLC

Contents

PART 3
Documents   97

Abbreviations

ARVN	Army of the Republic of Vietnam
CAPS	Combined action platoons
CIA	Central Intelligence Agency
CORDS	Civilian Operations and Revolutionary Development Support
COSVN	Central Office for South Vietnam
DMZ	demilitarized zone
DRV	Democratic Republic of Vietnam
ICP	Indochinese Communist Party
JCS	Joint Chiefs of Staff
MAAG	Military Assistance Advisory Group
MACV	Military Assistance Command, Vietnam
MIA	Missing in action
NCC	National Coordinating Committee to End the War in Vietnam
NLF	National Liberation Front
NVA	North Vietnamese Army
OSS	Office of Strategic Services
PAVN	People's Army of Vietnam
PLAF	People's Liberation Armed Forces
POW	Prisoner of War
PRG	People's Revolutionary Government
PROVN	Program for the Pacification and Long-Term Development of South Vietnam
RD	Revolutionary Development
RVNAF	Republic of Vietnam Armed Forces
SAM	Surface-to-air missile
SANE	Committee for a Sane Nuclear Policy
SDS	Students for a Democratic Society
SEATO	Southeast Asia Treaty Organization
US	United States
VC	Viet Cong
VNA	Vietnamese National Army
VNQDD	Vietnamese Nationalist Party
VVAW	Vietnam Veterans Against the War

Chronology

1941

May   Formation of the Viet Minh.

1945

2 September   Ho Chi Minh publicly declares a provisional government and Vietnamese national independence.

1946

23 November   French bombardment of Haiphong.

1949

October   Communists defeat Nationalists in Chinese Civil War.

1950

8 May   The United States agrees to provide France with military and economic assistance in Indochina.

1954

7 May   French forces surrender to the Viet Minh at Dien Bien Phu.

21 July   The Geneva Conference concludes with the signing of the Geneva Accords.

8 September   The Southeast Asia Treaty Organization (SEATO) is established.

1955

26 October   Ngo Dinh Diem is elected President of South Vietnam.

1956

20 July   United States supports Diem's refusal to hold national elections as the deadline established in the Geneva Accords passes.

1957

October   Small-scale civil war begins in South Vietnam between Diem's forces and communist-led insurgents.

1960

20 December   Formation of the National Liberation Front.

1962

6 February   United States establishes Military Assistance Command, Vietnam (MACV) with General Paul Harkins as commander of American armed forces.

1963

3 January   Battle of Ap Bac.

May–August   Buddhist-led demonstrations occur in South Vietnam's largest cities.

1 November   Ngo Dinh Diem is killed in a coup and replaced by Duong Van Minh.

December   North Vietnam sends its first NVA regular units into the South.

1964

30 January   Nguyen Khanh overthrows Duong Van Minh as head of South Vietnamese government.

20 June   General William Westmoreland succeeds General Paul Harkins as commander of MACV.

2 August   North Vietnamese patrol boats attack the *Maddox* in the Gulf of Tonkin near the North Vietnamese coast.

4–5 August   Both the *Maddox* and the *C. Turner Joy* report being under attack. US naval aircraft conduct reprisal raids against North Vietnamese targets.

7 August   US Congress passes the Gulf of Tonkin Resolution.

October   General Khanh resigns as South Vietnam's president and is replaced by Tran Van Huong.

1 November   NLF forces attack Bien Hoa Air Base.

1965

27–28   South Vietnamese President Tran Van Huong is ousted
January   and General Khanh returns to power.

7 February   NLF forces attack a US military base near Pleiku. President Johnson orders retaliatory air strikes against North Vietnamese targets.

13 February	President Johnson orders a sustained bombing campaign against North Vietnam known as Operation Rolling Thunder. Actual bombing begins on 2 March and continues, with occasional pauses, until 31 October 1968.
25 February	South Vietnam's Armed Forces Council replaces General Khanh as head of state with Air Marshal Nguyen Cao Ky.
8 March	The first US combat troops arrive in Vietnam.
6 April	President Johnson authorizes US forces to conduct offensive operations to support ARVN forces.
7 April	President Johnson's speech at Johns Hopkins University offers unconditional discussions with North Vietnam.
19 June	Air Marshal Ky becomes premier of the eighth South Vietnamese government since Diem was overthrown.
21–28 July	President Johnson makes a series of decisions that amount to committing the United States to a major war in Vietnam. Among the decisions he makes: draft calls will be raised to 35,000 per month; 50,000 additional troops will be sent to Vietnam with additional increases as the situation demands; and the air war against North Vietnam is expanded.
23 October–20 November	The battle of the Ia Drang Valley, the first major land battle between American and North Vietnamese regular forces.

1966

4 February	The US Senate Foreign Relations Committee, chaired by Senator J. William Fulbright, holds televised hearings on the Vietnam War.
6 February	President Johnson convenes a conference in Honolulu on the Vietnam War.
March–April	Buddhist and student protests against the Saigon government.

1967

8–26 January	Operation Cedar Falls takes place in the Iron Triangle region northeast of Saigon.
22 February–1 April	Operation Junction City takes place in War Zone C near the Cambodian border.
3 September	Nguyen Van Thieu is elected president of South Vietnam.

29 September	President Johnson offers to stop the bombing of North Vietnam if it will agree to start negotiations, known as the "San Antonio Formula."
16–21 October	Antiwar activists hold antidraft demonstrations throughout the United States; the largest occurs at the Army Induction Center in Oakland, California.
21–23 October	In the March on the Pentagon, 100,000 demonstrate in Washington DC against the Vietnam War.
30 November	Senator Eugene McCarthy announces his candidacy to challenge President Johnson for the Democratic presidential nomination in 1968.

1968

20 January– 14 April	North Vietnamese forces besiege an American Marine base at Khe Sanh.
30 January– 10 February	NLF and North Vietnamese forces launch the Tet Offensive against cities throughout South Vietnam.
20 February	Senate Foreign Relations Committee begins hearings on the 1964 Gulf of Tonkin incident.
28 February	General Earle Wheeler informs President Johnson that General Westmoreland needs an additional 206,000 troops.
12 March	Senator Eugene McCarthy pulls a near upset in the New Hampshire primary.
16 March	Senator Robert Kennedy announces his candidacy for the Democratic nomination on an antiwar platform.
16 March	A platoon of US soldiers slaughters hundreds of unarmed villagers in the hamlet of My Lai.
25–26 March	Johnson reconvenes the "Wise Men," who advise against additional troop increases and recommend a negotiated peace in Vietnam.
31 March	President Johnson announces a unilateral halt to all US bombing north of the 20th Parallel and that he will seek negotiations with North Vietnam. He also announces his withdrawal from the presidential race.
12 May	Peace negotiations between the United States and North Vietnam begin in Paris.
3 July	General Creighton Abrams formally succeeds General Westmoreland as Commander of US Military Assistance Command, Vietnam.

26–29 August	The Democratic National Convention in Chicago nominates Vice-President Hubert Humphrey for president. Riots occur between Chicago police and antiwar demonstrators.
31 October	President Johnson announces a complete halt to bombing over North Vietnam, ending Operation Rolling Thunder.

1969

25 January	The first four-way plenary session takes place in Paris among the United States, North Vietnam, South Vietnam, and the National Liberation Front.
18 March	President Nixon orders Operation Menu, the secret bombing of communist bases in Cambodia.
8 June	President Nixon announces that 25,000 US troops will be withdrawn by the end of August, the beginning of Vietnamization.
10 June	The NLF announces the formation of a Provisional Revolutionary Government (PRG) to challenge the Thieu government in South Vietnam.
4 August	Secret negotiations begin in Paris between US special envoy Henry Kissinger and North Vietnam's Xuan Thuy.
2 September	Ho Chi Minh dies.
15 October	The Moratorium, the largest antiwar demonstrations in American history, takes place across the country.
3 November	President Nixon's "silent majority" speech defends his Vietnam War policies.
15 November	The Mobilization draws more than 250,000 people to Washington DC in protest of the Vietnam War.

1970

18 March	General Lon Nol ousts Prince Norodom Sihanouk as Cambodia's head of state.
27 March	ARVN forces attack communist bases inside Cambodia for the first time.
30 April	American forces invade the Fishhook region of Cambodia.
4 May	Ohio National Guard troops fire into a crowd of student demonstrators on the campus of Kent State University, killing four and wounding nine.

9 May	An estimated 80,000 young people, mostly college students, demonstrate peacefully in the nation's capital, protesting the "Kent State Massacre" and calling for the immediate withdrawal of all US troops from Indochina.
20 May	More than 100,000 workers in New York City march in support of Nixon's war policies.
24 June	The US Senate repeals the Gulf of Tonkin Resolution.
30 June	US ground forces end their role in the Cambodian operation.
19 August	The United States signs a pact with Cambodia to provide Lon Nol's government with military aid.

1971

1 January	Congress forbids the use of US ground troops in either Laos or Cambodia.
8 February–24 March	South Vietnamese forces invade Laos to cut supply routes down the Ho Chi Minh Trail. Communist counterattacks drive them out of Laos and inflict heavy casualties.
29 March	Lieutenant William Calley is convicted of mass murder for his actions at My Lai. His sentence is later reduced and he is paroled after three years.
19–23 April	Vietnam Veterans Against the War stage a demonstration in Washington DC.
13 June	The *New York Times* begins publication of what comes to be referred to as *The Pentagon Papers*.
3 October	Nguyen Van Thieu is re-elected president of South Vietnam.
26 December	President Nixon orders the resumption of US bombing of North Vietnam.

1972

21–27 February	President Nixon makes his historic visit to China.
30 March–8 April	North Vietnam conducts its Easter Offensive, a three-pronged attack across the demilitarized zone, into the central highlands, and northwest of Saigon.
8 May	Nixon orders the mining of all North Vietnamese ports and the Linebacker bombing campaign.
20 May	President Nixon and Leonid Brezhnev meet in Moscow for a summit conference.

June	General Frederick Weyand replaces General Creighton Abrams as commander of US forces in Vietnam.
15 September	South Vietnamese forces recapture Quang Tri City.
8–11 October	Secret meetings in Paris between Henry Kissinger and Le Duc Tho produce a tentative settlement of the war.
22 October	President Thieu rejects the proposed settlement.
14 December	The US breaks off peace talks with the North Vietnamese.
18–31 December	President Nixon orders renewed mining of North Vietnamese harbors and Linebacker II bombing campaign, known as the "Christmas Bombing."
28 December	Hanoi announces its willingness to resume negotiations if the United States will stop bombing above the 20th Parallel. The bombing ends on 31 December.

1973

8–18 January	Henry Kissinger and Le Duc Tho resume negotiations in Paris, and reach an agreement similar to the one reached the previous October.
23 January	President Nixon announces the signing of the Paris Agreement, which goes into effect on 27 January 1973.
27 January	The US military draft ends.
1 February	Secret letter from Richard Nixon to Pham Van Dong promises postwar reconstruction aid to North Vietnam.
12 February	The release of US prisoners of war begins.
21 February	A cease-fire formally ends the 20-year war in Laos.
29 March	The last US combat troops and POWs leave South Vietnam.
4 June– 15 August	US Congress blocks all funds for any American military activities in Indochina. The Nixon administration works out a compromise to permit continued US bombing in Cambodia until 15 August.
14 August	US bombing of Cambodia ends.
7 November	Congress enacts the War Powers Act over President Nixon's veto.

1974

February	South Vietnam launches a military offensive against PRG-controlled areas west of Saigon.
9 August	Richard Nixon resigns the US presidency. Gerald Ford is sworn in as president.
16 September	President Ford offers clemency to draft evaders and deserters.

1975

6 January	NVA forces overrun Phuoc Long province. When the United States does not react, Hanoi concludes that America will not reintroduce its military forces to save South Vietnam.
28 January	President Ford requests an additional $722 million in military aid for South Vietnam. Congress refuses his request.
March	NVA forces launch an offensive in the central highlands.
12 March	Ban Me Thuot falls to the communists.
14 March	President Thieu orders the withdrawal of ARVN from the central highlands.
25 March	Hanoi launches its Ho Chi Minh campaign to "liberate" South Vietnam before the rainy season begins.
8–21 April	Communists win the last major battle of the Vietnam War at Xuan Loc, about 30 miles from Saigon.
12 April	President Nguyen Van Thieu resigns and flees South Vietnam.
17 April	The Khmer Rouge accepts the Cambodian government's surrender and occupies the capital city of Phnom Penh.
29–30 April	The last Americans and thousands of South Vietnamese are evacuated from Saigon.
30 April	Saigon falls to communist forces, ending the Vietnam War.

Who's Who

Abrams, Creighton (1914–74): Commander, US Military Assistance Command, Vietnam, 1968–72.

Agnew, Spiro (1918–96): Vice-President of the United States, 1969–74.

Ball, George (1909–94): US Undersecretary of State, 1961–66.

Bao Dai (1913–97): Emperor of Vietnam, 1926–45; abdicated 25 August, 1945; chief of state, State of Vietnam 1950–55.

Bay Vien (1904–70): Le Van "Bay" Vien headed the Binh Xuyen criminal enterprise. General in Vietnamese National Army. Fled to France after losing the Battle of Saigon in 1954.

Brown, Sam (1943–): US political activist; coordinator, Vietnam Moratorium Committee, 1969–70.

Bui Diem (1923–): Republic of Vietnam ambassador to the United States, 1967–72.

Bundy, McGeorge (1919–96): National Security Adviser, 1961–66.

Bunker, Ellsworth (1894–1994): US ambassador to the Republic of Vietnam, 1967–73.

Bush, George H.W. (1924–): President of the United States, 1989–92.

Calley, William (1943–): US Army Lieutenant, platoon leader convicted of My Lai Massacre.

Caputo, Philip (1943–): US Marine Lieutenant, author of *A Rumor of War*.

Carter, Jimmy (1924–): President of the United States, 1977–81.

Chennault, Anna (1925–): Chinese-born Republican Party activist.

Chiang Kai-shek (1887–1975): Chinese general and leader of the Nationalist government in China; President of the Republic of China on Taiwan, 1949–75.

Clifford, Clark (1906–98): US Secretary of Defense, 1968–69.

Clinton, Bill (1946–): US Governor of Arkansas, 1979–81, 1983–92; President of the United States, 1993–2000.

Collins, Joseph Lawton (1896–1987): US General; Special Ambassador to Vietnam, 1954.

Cronkite, Walter (1916–2009): US television news reporter and anchorman, 1962–81.

d'Argenlieu, Georges Thierry (1889–1964): French High Commissioner of Indochina, 1945–47.

de Lattre de Tassigny, Jean (1889–1952): French High Commissioner and Commander of French military forces in Indochina, 1950–51.

Dulles, John Foster (1888–1959): US Secretary of State, 1953–59.

Duong Van Minh (1916–2001): Republic of Vietnam general and political leader, head of state, 1963–64, 1975.

Eisenhower, Dwight (1890–1969): President of the United States, 1953–60.

Ellsberg, Daniel (1931–): US intelligence analyst for RAND Corporation and US Defense Department; leaked *The Pentagon Papers* to the *New York Times* in 1971.

Ford, Gerald (1913–2006): US Congressman, 1949–73; Vice-President, 1973–74; President of the United States, 1974–76.

Fulbright, J. William (1905–95): US Senator, 1945–74; chaired Senate Foreign Relations Committee, 1959–74.

Goldwater, Barry (1909–98): US Senator, 1952–65, 1969–84; Republican candidate for president, 1964.

Harkins, Paul (1904–84): Commander, US Military Assistance Command, Vietnam, 1962–64.

Harriman, Averell (1891–1986): US Assistant Secretary of State, 1962–64; Ambassador-at-large, 1960–61, 1965–69.

Heng Samrin (1934–): Cambodian communist revolutionary; head of state, Cambodia, 1979–91.

Ho Chi Minh (1890–1969): Vietnamese communist revolutionary, President, Democratic Republic of Vietnam, 1945–69.

Humphrey, Hubert (1911–78): US Senator, 1949–64, 1970–78; Vice-President, 1965–68; Democratic candidate for president, 1968.

Johnson, Harold (1912–83): Chief of Staff, US Army, 1964–68.

Johnson, Lyndon (1908–73): US Congressman, 1937–48; Senator, 1949–60; Vice-President, 1961–63; President of the United States, 1963–68.

Kennedy, John (1917–63): US Congressman, 1946–53; Senator, 1953–60; President of the United States, 1961–63.

Kennedy, Robert (1925–68): US Attorney General, 1961–64; Senator, 1965–68; presidential candidate, 1968.

Khrushchev, Nikita (1894–1971): First Secretary, Communist Party of the Soviet Union, 1953–64; Premier of the Soviet Union, 1958–64.

King, Martin Luther, Jr (1929–68): US civil rights and antiwar activist.

Kissinger, Henry (1923–): US National Security Adviser, 1969–73; Secretary of State, 1973–77.

Krulak, Victor (1913–2008): US Marine General; Commanding General, Fleet Marine Force, Pacific, 1964–68.

Laird, Melvin (1922–2016): US Secretary of Defense, 1969–73.

Lansdale, Edward (1908–87): US Major General; expert in counterinsurgency; key American advisor to Ngo Dinh Diem in mid-1950s.

Le Duan (1907–86): Secretary General, Communist Party of Vietnam, 1959–69; Head, Communist Party of Vietnam, 1969–86.

Le Duc Tho (1910–90): Influential member of Communist Party of Vietnam; Chief DRV negotiator at Paris Peace Talks, 1968–73.

Lodge, Henry Cabot, Jr (1902–85): US ambassador to Republic of Vietnam, 1963–64, 1965–67.

Lon Nol (1913–85): Cambodian military officer; Prime Minister of Cambodia, 1970–72; President of Khmer Republic, 1972–75.

Mansfield, Mike (1903–2001): US Senator, 1952–77.

Mao Zedong (1893–1976): Marxist theoretician; Chinese Communist Party chairman, 1935–76; chief of state, People's Republic of China, 1949–59.

Martin, Graham (1912–90): US ambassador to Republic of Vietnam, 1973–75.

McCarthy, Eugene (1916–2005): US Congressman, 1948–58; Senator, 1959–70; presidential candidate, 1968.

McCone, John (1902–91): Director of US Central Intelligence Agency, 1961–65.

McNamara, Robert (1916–2009): US Secretary of Defense, 1961–68.

McNaughton, John (1921–67): US Department of Defense staff; Assistant Secretary of Defense for International Security Affairs, 1964–67.

Mendès-France, Pierre (1907–82): French Premier, 1954–55; helped broker the 1954 Geneva Accords.

Moyers, Bill (1934–): US White House chief of staff, 1964–65; press secretary, 1965–66.

Navarre, Henri (1898–1983): Commander of French military forces in Indochina, 1953–54.

Ngo Dinh Diem (1901–63): President of the Republic of Vietnam, 1954–63.

Ngo Dinh Nhu (1910–63): Head of Can Lao Party and secret police in the Republic of Vietnam; younger brother of Ngo Dinh Diem.

Nguyen Cao Ky (1930–2011): Commander, Republic of Vietnam Air Force; Premier, Republic of Vietnam, 1965–67; Vice-President, 1967–71.

Nguyen Chanh Thi (1923–2007): General, Army of the Republic of Vietnam; Commander of I Corps whose removal led to Buddhist protests in 1966.

Nguyen Chi Thanh (1914–67): General, People's Army of Vietnam; Director, Central Office for South Vietnam (COSVN), 1965–67.

Nguyen Khanh (1927–2013): General, Army of the Republic of Vietnam; Premier, Republic of Vietnam, 1965.

Nguyen Van Hinh (1915–2004): General, Army of the Republic of Vietnam; led failed coup against Ngo Dinh Diem, October 1954.

Nguyen Van Thieu (1923–2001): General, Army of the Republic of Vietnam; President, Republic of Vietnam, 1967–75.

Nixon, Richard (1913–94): US Congressman, 1947–51; Senator, 1951–53; Vice-President, 1953–60; President of the United States, 1969–74.

Pearson, Lester (1897–1972): Prime Minister of Canada, 1963–68.

Pham Van Dong (1906–2000): Vietnamese communist revolutionary; Premier, Democratic Republic of Vietnam, 1950–75.

Phan Boi Chau (1867–1940): Vietnamese nationalist and political activist.

Phan Huy Quat (1909–79): Vietnamese political figure; Minister of Defense, State of Vietnam, 1950–54; Minister of Foreign Affairs, Republic of Vietnam, 1964; Premier, Republic of Vietnam, 1965.

Pol Pot (1928–98): Cambodian communist revolutionary; founder of Khmer Rouge, 1963; Prime Minister, Democratic Kampuchea, 1976–78; head of Khmer Rouge military forces, 1963–85.

Reagan, Ronald (1911–2004): US Governor of California, 1967–75; President of the United States, 1981–88.

Rogers, William (1913–2001): US Secretary of State, 1969–73.

Roosevelt, Franklin (1882–1945): US Governor of New York, 1928–32; President of the United States, 1933–45.

Rostow, Walt (1916–2003): US State Department staff, 1961–66; special assistant to the president for national security affairs, 1966–69.

Rusk, Dean (1909–94): US Secretary of State, 1961–69.

Sainteny, Jean (1907–78): French diplomat who concluded Ho–Sainteny agreement, 1946; senior French delegate to the Democratic Republic of Vietnam, 1954–58.

Salisbury, Harrison (1908–93): US journalist with the *New York Times*, 1949–73.

Sharp, Ulysses S. Grant, Jr (1906–2001): US Navy Admiral, Commander-in-Chief of the Pacific Command, 1964–68.

Sihanouk, Norodom (1922–2012): Leading Cambodian political figure; head of state, Cambodia, 1960–70.

Souvanna Phouma (1901–84): Prime Minister of Laos, 1951–54, 1956–58, 1960–75.

Taylor, Maxwell (1901–87): US Army Chief of Staff, 1955–59; Military representative of the president, 1961–62; Chairman, Joint Chiefs of Staff, 1962–64; ambassador to the Republic of Vietnam, 1964–65.

Thich Quang Duc (1897–1963): Buddhist monk whose self-immolation in 1963 attracted world attention.

Tran Van Huong (1903–82): Prime Minister of the Republic of Vietnam, 1964–65, 1968–69; Vice-President, 1971–75.

Truman, Harry (1884–1972): US Senator, 1934–44; Vice-President, 1944–45; President of the United States, 1945–52.

U Thant (1909–74): Burmese ambassador to the United Nations; Secretary-General of the United Nations General Assembly, 1962–72.

Vann, John Paul (1924–72): US Army Lieutenant Colonel, 1961–63; pacification representative of the Agency for International Development, 1965–72.

Vo Nguyen Giap (1911–2013): Leading Vietnamese military strategist, primary military commander of the Democratic Republic of Vietnam, 1944–75.

Westmoreland, William (1914–2005): US Army General: Commander, Military Assistance Command, Vietnam, 1964–68; Army Chief of Staff, 1968–72.

Weyand, Frederick (1916–2010): US Army General; Commander, Military Assistance Command, Vietnam, 1972–73; Army Chief of Staff, 1974–76.

Wheeler, Earle (1908–75): US Army Chief of Staff, 1962–64; Chairman, Joint Chiefs of Staff, 1964–70.

Glossary

Agrovilles Failed 1959–61 effort of South Vietnamese President Diem to separate peasants from the NLF. Designed to relocate rural villagers to fortified settlements, the agrovilles disrupted and antagonized the peasants, failed to provide adequate security, and collapsed from government corruption and popular resistance.

Attrition US military strategy in Vietnam which measured progress through the body count rather than control of territory. Advocated by General William Westmoreland to maintain the infantry's traditional role of making contact and destroying enemy forces. Attrition assumed victory would come when the enemy lost more soldiers than it could replace. It failed largely because it tried to impose a conventional war on a guerrilla conflict and underestimated the Vietnamese capacity to absorb losses.

Central Office for South Vietnam (COSVN) Vietnamese communist headquarters that controlled the war effort in the South. Consisted of a relatively few officers and staff in a jungle hideaway that moved frequently to avoid detection or capture. Usually located in Tay Ninh province near the Cambodian border.

Containment policy United States Cold War policy designed to restrict communist expansion. Containment grew out of ideas expressed by US diplomat George Kennan in 1946–47. He believed that patient but firm resistance to Soviet expansion would ultimately end its aggression. Kennan later indicated that he favored political responses, though US presidents from Harry Truman to George Bush often utilized military force.

Counterinsurgency Efforts by an established government to defeat a rebellion aimed at overthrowing its authority. Vietnamese rebels, or insurgents, used guerrilla tactics to undermine the Saigon government and gain political control. Successful counterinsurgency provides security for and gains control of the general population upon which the guerrillas must rely.

Crossover point The theoretical point in time when the United States and its allies inflicted more casualties on North Vietnamese and NLF forces than they could replace through recruitment. Some US officials believed that upon reaching this point, the enemy would be forced to end the war on terms favorable to the United States, but the crossover point was never achieved.

DeSoto missions Electronic intelligence-gathering conducted during 1963–64 by the US Navy. These missions often consisted of intercepting North Vietnamese communications during South Vietnamese raids into the North. One such mission, involving the US destroyer *Maddox*, resulted in the Gulf of Tonkin incident.

Détente Means "lessening of tension." Refers to a period from the late 1960s to the early 1970s when Cold War tensions between the United States and Soviet Union were reduced, but not ended. Highlighted by President Richard Nixon's trips to the Soviet Union and China, *détente* featured limited cooperation and negotiations rather than confrontation.

Doi moi Meaning "renovation," it refers to the economic and political liberalization implemented by the Vietnamese leadership in 1986. This was a response to the damaged and struggling economy that was evident by the end of the 1970s. The reforms focused on reducing economic centralization, but also included some lessening of political censorship.

Domino theory Cold War era view of some US officials that the fall of one country to communism would lead to a chain reaction collapse of its neighbors. Served as an important argument in developing the containment policy. In the case of Southeast Asia, believers feared that the loss of South Vietnam could spread communist control as far as Japan, the Philippines, India, and Indonesia. The theory faded after the Vietnam War.

Enclave strategy Military strategy briefly adopted by the United States in March 1965. American combat forces were limited to protecting a number of heavily populated coastal regions and military bases, enclaves, while South Vietnamese forces took the offensive in the countryside. With American protection of key areas, the South would have time to build up its military and political strength. Pressure from US military leaders and ARVN's poor performance ended the enclave strategy in June.

Montagnards The native peoples of the Indochina highlands. In Vietnam they numbered around one million people divided into perhaps 30 tribes. They retained a culture ethnically distinct from the Vietnamese majority who settled on the coast or in the river valleys. Montagnards were generally viewed by ethnic Vietnamese as uncivilized and faced discriminatory treatment. In both Vietnam and Laos they often allied themselves with the United States.

OPLAN 34A Commando raids conducted by South Vietnamese or mercenary troops along the North Vietnamese coastline. Designed to harass the North Vietnamese and collect intelligence, they were often supported by US DeSoto missions. They were first approved in late 1963.

Pacification   The effort of a government to extend its control into insurgent areas. Typically these efforts include providing food, medical aid, and political reforms, but emphasize physical security. Saigon and US officials tried to provide security and political and economic stability to South Vietnamese villagers through programs such as the Strategic Hamlet Program, CORDS, and the Phoenix Program.

Search and destroy   Name given to the US tactical application of its attrition strategy in Vietnam. It represented the dominant tactical approach used by American forces in the war. US forces took the offensive to locate, engage, and destroy enemy forces. This assumed that American firepower could inflict sufficient casualties to force the enemy to give up its fight.

Strategic hamlets   A 1961–64 program, similar to agrovilles, that President Diem used to limit the effectiveness of the NLF. Based somewhat on the suggestions of British advisor Robert Thompson, Diem tried to build fortified hamlets that, with the aid of regular military units, could defend themselves from insurgents. Like similar efforts, the strategic hamlets were poorly implemented and failed to achieve their goals.

Viet Minh   Communist front organization founded in 1941 by the Indochinese Communist Party. It served as the primary organization for developing a broad nationalist program against foreign occupation. The Viet Minh de-emphasized the communist social revolution to attract the broadest possible coalition. The Viet Minh seized power during the 1945 August Revolution. The organization's full name was Viet Nam Doc Lap Dong Minh Hoi.

Vietnamization   The name given to President Richard Nixon's policy of gradually returning the primary responsibility for conducting the war to the South Vietnamese. As US troops withdrew, South Vietnamese forces were increased in size and received additional training and equipment. Southern forces focused on both offensive operations and village defense against the communist infrastructure.

Wise Men   Informal advisors to President Lyndon Johnson who included some of America's most respected leaders; for example, Dean Acheson, General Omar Bradley, and Henry Cabot Lodge, Jr. In November 1967 they reaffirmed Johnson's policy, but in March 1968, after the Tet Offensive, a majority counseled military de-escalation.

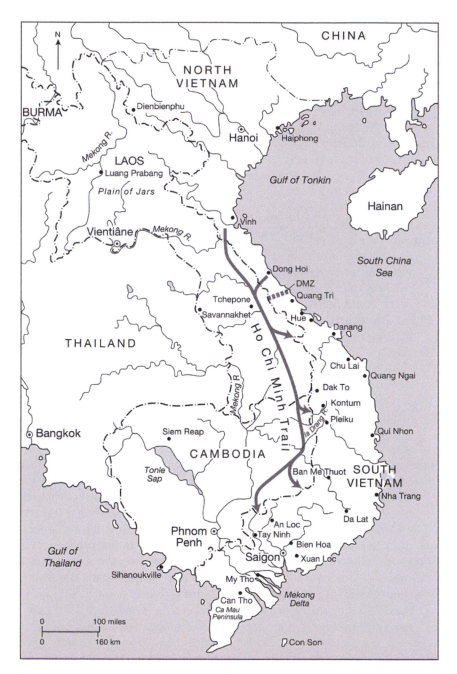

Map 1 Indochina

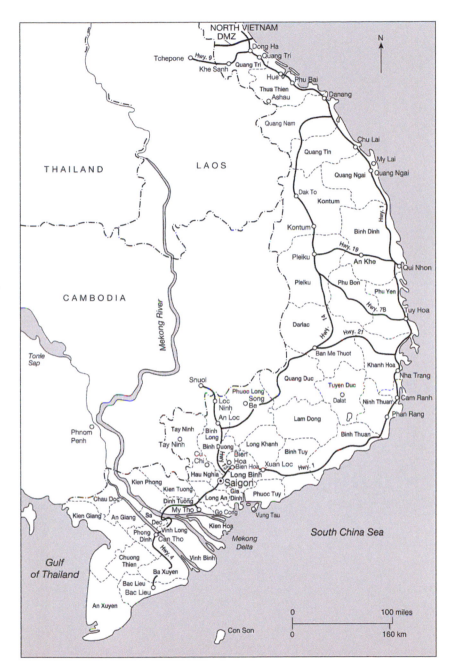

Map 2 South Vietnam

Part 1
The Background

1 Roots of the Vietnam War

It is ironic that Vietnam and the United States engaged in such a long and bitter war. They had collaborated during World War II, and US officials listened as **Ho Chi Minh** quoted Thomas Jefferson in the Vietnamese Declaration of Independence. Vietnam looked to the United States for moral and material aid as it sought liberation from French colonialism. In the end, however, the growing Cold War made it virtually impossible for American policy-makers to see beyond the communist doctrine espoused by the Vietnamese nationalists' most influential leaders. Americans viewed the struggle in Vietnam as part of a new global conflict against communism, while the Vietnamese saw the war against the United States as the latest phase of a long fight for independence.

The Rise of Vietnamese Nationalism

Vietnam's intense nationalism developed through centuries of resisting foreign intrusion. As a kingdom in Southeast Asia's Red River Valley, Vietnam was conquered by the Chinese in 111 BC. Although they borrowed important aspects of Chinese culture, the Vietnamese retained a fierce sense of their own identity. After numerous unsuccessful rebellions, the Vietnamese finally ended 1,000 years of Chinese domination in 939 AD. Except for a brief return to Chinese rule from 1407 to 1428, they successfully resisted invasions from the Chinese and Mongol empires in the north and from Champa and Cambodia in the south. The Vietnamese themselves expanded southward, conquering Champa by 1471 and finally taking the Mekong River delta from the crumbling Cambodian empire during the early 1700s. Although divided by the competing Trinh and Nguyen families in 1620, Vietnam was reunified within its modern boundaries in 1802.

European expansion provided the next threat to Vietnamese independence. Portuguese contact with Vietnam dates from 1516, and the French followed in 1615. Establishing a military presence in 1858 to support economic exploitation and missionary activity, France ultimately gained control of the entire country by 1883, dividing it into three regions: Cochin China (south), Annam (central), and Tonkin (north). Annexing neighboring Cambodia and Laos as well, by 1893 France established the Indochinese Union governed from Hanoi. Although a minority of Vietnam's traditional mandarin ruling class allied its interests to the French presence, the majority of the population suffered economically and politically under French rule.

Resistance to French colonialism began almost immediately. French political and economic policies prevented the emergence of a strong middle class or liberal political parties, which drove most nationalist movements toward revolutionary activity. While the earliest revolts planned to return power to the mandarin class, twentieth-century rebellions shifted their ideology toward modern western institutions and technology. The most influential of these early nationalists was **Phan Boi Chau**, whose Modernization Society fought the French with propaganda, demonstrations, and violence, but declined after World War I. The Constitutionalist Party of the 1920s pursued reforms through collaboration, but its failures encouraged further clandestine efforts. The Vietnamese Nationalist Party (VNQDD) formed in 1927 around upper- and middle-class intellectuals. Although they infiltrated native garrisons, a planned military revolt in February 1930 was quickly suppressed. The resulting French reprisals decimated the VNQDD's leadership and drove its remnants into China.

Ultimately the Indochinese Communist Party developed into the most successful nationalist organization. Ho Chi Minh, born Nguyen Tat Thanh and previously known as Nguyen Ai Quoc, emerged as the most revered leader in Vietnam. As a seaman, Ho left Vietnam in 1911 and would not return until 30 years later. He traveled the world, including to the United States, before moving to Paris at the end of World War I, where he became active in the sizeable Vietnamese community. His appeal to the postwar Versailles peace conference for national self-determination was ignored by the major powers, but earned him a leading role in the Vietnamese nationalist movement. Disappointed at the West's response and influenced by the writings of Vladimir Lenin, Ho joined the French Communist Party as a means of working toward Vietnam's eventual independence. He moved to Moscow in 1923 for study, then proceeded to China the following year to build a revolutionary movement for Indochina. In February 1930, Ho was among the founders of the Vietnamese Communist Party, later renamed the Indochinese Communist Party (ICP). The party supported peasant revolts in the fall of 1930, but the French again suppressed the rebellion by the following spring. The ICP suffered serious losses and its surviving leaders scattered beyond Vietnam's borders. By the mid-1930s, however, the ICP regained its position as an important nationalist organization, and attempted to participate in a broad national front against the French.

The events of World War II had a dramatic impact on the course of Vietnamese history. France, having already surrendered to Germany in

June 1940, conceded control over Indochina to Japanese expansion later that year, though Japan permitted the French political administration to remain in place. Communist efforts to exploit the situation through an uprising in southern Vietnam failed, and the French executed several key leaders. ICP leaders in the north withdrew to the mountains in the face of Japanese advances. From southern China, Ho Chi Minh helped establish a united front organization in which the ICP played the dominant, though secret, role. The Viet Nam Doc Lap Dong Minh, more commonly called the **Viet Minh,** formed in May 1941 and appealed to both moderates and radicals through its emphasis on both national independence and social reform.

Fearing that France, now liberated from German control, might undermine their position, the Japanese overthrew the French colonial structure in March 1945 and established a collaborative Vietnamese government under Emperor **Bao Dai.** The collapse of the French system resulted in a vacuum of authority, especially in rural areas, which allowed the Viet Minh to establish control of six northern provinces. A devastating famine further eroded government authority, and when the Japanese suddenly surrendered in August, the Viet Minh called for a general uprising to create an independent state. During this August Revolution, the Viet Minh met with little opposition in taking power throughout much of the northern and central provinces, and forced Bao Dai to abdicate from his palace in Hue. Having prevailed in much of the country, on 2 September before a Hanoi crowd of a half-million people, Ho Chi Minh called for allied recognition of the newly proclaimed Democratic Republic of Vietnam (DRV) [**Doc. 5**].

Although the Viet Minh had made impressive gains, it faced challenges to the organization's legitimacy. Effective competition from other nationalist organizations and the Cao Dai and Hoa Hao religious sects limited their influence in Cochin China. Just as importantly, the allies designated China and Great Britain to accept the Japanese surrender in northern and southern Indochina respectively, and to occupy the region until stable government had been restored. Their arrival, combined with their governments' recognition of French claims, undermined Viet Minh authority. When British troops arrived in Saigon that September, they joined with French forces to drive armed Vietnamese out of the city. Military attacks and reprisals took place from both sides. As the broadly based Committee of the South opened a guerrilla war against the French in the South, France prepared to reassert its authority in the North as well.

The United States responded to Vietnamese efforts inconsistently. President **Franklin Roosevelt** initially opposed France's reassertion of control after the war, preferring a trusteeship followed by independence [**Doc. 4**]. During 1945, the Viet Minh provided intelligence to the American Office of Strategic Services (OSS) and received both weapons and training in return. Ho sought US support for his political goals, but Washington ignored his appeals. By the end of the war President **Harry Truman** and other American officials were more concerned with restoring French power as an ally against the Soviet Union and opposed Ho's communist beliefs.

The First Indochina War

Faced with a rising tide of Vietnamese nationalism, France appointed as its high commissioner for Indochina Admiral **Georges Thierry d'Argenlieu**, who initiated a military campaign against the Viet Minh in October 1945. By February 1946 he had re-established control of southern Vietnam, while at the same time negotiating political differences with the Vietnamese.

In the face of French military actions, Ho Chi Minh recognized the need to bargain for Vietnam's future, but remained flexible in pursuing his political goals. The Viet Minh was especially concerned with China's occupation of the North because of **Chiang Kai-shek**'s support for their political rivals and, as future South Vietnamese ambassador to the United States, **Bui Diem**, remarked, "The Chinese looked as if they would steal anything not tied down" (Bui Diem, 1987: 39). Though criticized by Viet Minh militants, in November 1945 Ho dissolved the ICP and integrated smaller nationalist parties into a National Assembly governing the North to build a more broadly based united front that could attract foreign aid. He also opened negotiations in Hanoi with French diplomat **Jean Sainteny** in October 1945, but lost significant leverage in February when a Chinese agreement to withdraw its troops signified a quick return of French military forces to the North. They reached a preliminary deal on 6 March 1946. The Ho–Sainteny agreement recognized the Democratic Republic of Vietnam (DRV) as a free state within the French Union, and called for referendums in Cochin China, Annam, and Tonkin to resolve their permanent political status. In return, the Vietnamese agreed to accept a substantial French military force for five years to replace the Chinese.

Viet Minh nationalists viewed this as a step toward unification rather than a permanent solution and negotiations continued. While Ho traveled to Paris to discuss implementing the March agreement, however, on 1 June d'Argenlieu undermined the talks by unilaterally recognizing Cochin China as an autonomous republic. Events in Vietnam moved forward without official sanction from Paris. With the new French government uninterested in compromise, Ho's two months of negotiations ended with political issues left unresolved. He struck a last-minute modus vivendi in mid-September 1946 that offered little except a cease-fire and future talks. Ho returned to Hanoi in October where, despite continued criticism from militants, the National Assembly elected him president of the DRV.

Without strong direction from Paris, France's Indochina policy fell largely to officials in Vietnam and drifted toward war. Both sides competed throughout the country for the authority to govern, but a tenuous cease-fire fell apart late in the year. Skirmishing in the North erupted into war when a French ship bombarded Haiphong in late November. Days later French military forces attacked throughout the city and thousands of Vietnamese died under naval, air, and artillery fire. Fighting spread, and by the end of the year French forces controlled Hanoi and were driving the Viet Minh into the countryside. The United States offered mediation, but viewed the communist-dominated Viet Minh as an unacceptable replacement for French colonialism. The State Department's inability to see beyond the Cold War was evident in a 1948 report that concluded "we cannot afford to assume that Ho is anything but Moscow-directed" (Hess, 1987: 317).

General **Vo Nguyen Giap**, the Viet Minh's leading military strategist, frustrated French hopes for a swift victory by avoiding major battles when possible. Recognizing his technological disadvantages, he relied on a protracted war strategy to wear the enemy down. Early French gains in 1947 bogged down during the summer monsoon season, when the rudimentary road system in Vietnam made mechanized warfare extremely difficult. French military operations later that year failed to achieve their goals of capturing the Viet Minh leaders and crippling their military forces. The Viet Minh absorbed heavy blows, but slipped away and returned to their bases once the French had pulled back into the Red River delta. The stalemate remained.

Concerns about the costs and length of an Indochina war led France to search for an alternative solution. Although the French controlled the major cities, the Viet Minh held much of rural northern and central Vietnam, and their influence was increasing. The departure of Chinese forces had weakened noncommunist Vietnamese nationalist groups that had enjoyed their support. The Viet Minh suppressed their nationalist rivals and engaged in political indoctrination, supplemented when deemed necessary by terrorism and targeted assassinations (Logevall, 2012: 172).

France hoped to end the war and undermine Viet Minh legitimacy by establishing a rival anticommunist government. French officials tried to entice Bao Dai to return as head of a nationalist government that could allow continued French control. Initially, Bao Dai negotiated for complete independence from France, but ultimately accepted the Elysée Agreements on 8 March 1949. These established the former emperor as head of the State of Vietnam and granted limited independence within the French Union, but left France in control of Vietnam's finances, diplomacy, and military affairs. This "Bao Dai Solution" offered the necessary veneer to disguise French domination. By accepting what was essentially the French position, however, Bao Dai generated little enthusiasm among Vietnamese and drew criticism from the Viet Minh and other nationalists.

American interest in Vietnam increased as the Cold War intensified. The United States' traditional stance against colonialism initially tempered its support for France in Indochina. At first, this appeared to be a reasonable response, since the Viet Minh received little external support from either the Soviet Union or the West through 1947. The United States ignored Ho Chi Minh's appeals for mediation, aid, or trade, and the long-term survival of the Viet Minh depended on its ability to persuade both the Vietnamese people and foreign powers that it represented the only legitimate government in Vietnam. By 1947, however, US leaders perceived that the Soviets presented a global threat to national security. Their response was the **containment policy**, initially applied to Europe, but later expanded to other parts of the world. The growing conflict in Vietnam, with its communist component, made it part of the Cold War struggle. Although publicly supporting France's war to block the Viet Minh and communist expansion, knowledgeable Americans privately remained doubtful about the chances of France or Bao Dai to undermine support for Ho Chi Minh's government.

The United States nevertheless escalated its commitment to the French in Vietnam in the wake of new circumstances. The United States lost its nuclear monopoly in August 1949 when the Soviet Union successfully exploded an atomic bomb. Only a month later, **Mao Zedong**'s communist forces defeated Chiang Kai-shek to end the lengthy Chinese civil war. American fears that these events would affect Indochina appeared confirmed when China recognized Ho Chi Minh's government on 18 January 1950, and the Soviet Union followed by the end of the month. French officials shrewdly recast the French–Indochina War from a localized war for empire to an effort to defeat global communism. The United States applied less pressure to the French for Vietnamese independence and formally recognized Bao Dai's government in February 1950 as the only alternative to Ho Chi Minh. The outbreak of the Korean War in August further hardened America's Cold War position. These events led to a significant US commitment to military spending for Indochina and provided greater urgency for military involvement in Vietnam. They also solidified American policy-makers' perceptions of the French–Viet Minh war as part of a communist effort to grab the entire region. Some officials applied the term **domino theory** to the view that Vietnam's fall would quickly lead to communist domination of all Southeast Asia. The possibility of that outcome in Vietnam outweighed US concerns about supporting French colonialism.

During 1950 the fighting in Vietnam intensified. Despite French dominance in air and sea power, by that fall Chinese military advisors, supplies, and equipment allowed Giap's ground troops to reach a rough parity. During the first half of 1950, French military efforts inflicted heavy losses on the Viet Minh in Cochin China, and thereafter the war played out primarily in the North. French efforts to pacify the Red River delta achieved initial success as well. In the fall, however, French forces suffered a major setback and abandoned a number of isolated posts close to the Chinese border. Although the Viet Minh also took heavy casualties, French control in Tonkin was now effectively limited to the Red River delta. French losses necessitated creation of a Vietnamese National Army to provide both needed manpower and an indigenous force to add legitimacy to Bao Dai's government.

The following year French prospects improved. Much needed American aid increased after the Korean War began, and the United States established the Military Assistance Advisory Group (MAAG) to facilitate the arrival of supplies and equipment. In December 1950, the Paris government appointed military hero **Jean de Lattre de Tassigny** as commander-in-chief of the Expeditionary Corps and high commissioner for Indochina. De Lattre's arrival boosted French morale. When General Giap launched a series of offensives in the early months of 1951 to penetrate the Red River delta, the French prevailed at each point of attack, inflicting heavy losses and forcing the Viet Minh to abandon large unit assaults and return to guerilla warfare. By the end of 1951, the French built a fortified "De Lattre Line" to defend the Red River delta, but their success was only temporary. De Lattre himself left Vietnam in mid-November 1951 and succumbed to cancer in early 1952. His death drained much of France's remaining enthusiasm for the war.

France also waged a political war in an uphill struggle to keep Indochina under its supervision. It sought to acquire additional US aid by arguing that Vietnam and Korea were two elements of a single global confrontation, but the Americans insisted they would not contribute ground troops to another Asian land war. By 1952, the French faced the dilemma of being almost completely reliant upon US aid for its Indochina war, but resisting American efforts to participate in actual decision-making. At the same time, the United States possessed limited leverage because of its need of French support in building a European defensive alliance. The French could not afford to maintain adequate military forces in Indochina while building up a large army for defense in Europe and wanted to negotiate an exit from Indochina in spring 1952. The United States, however, pressed them to continue fighting until they held an advantage that would permit an acceptable settlement.

French and Viet Minh forces continued to trade victories. In mid-October 1952, a Viet Minh campaign captured French outposts north and west of Hanoi, inflicting heavy losses and damaging morale. As one French officer reflected, "It looks as though from now on the Indo-Chinese war is to be a permanent nightmare" (Logevall, 2012: 323). France responded with Operation Lorraine at the end of October, its largest offensive ever in Vietnam. Despite early success, French forces failed to engage Giap's main forces, became overextended, and retreated again to the delta defense perimeter. Overconfidence led Giap to counterattack the following month with another large unit assault on Na San to the west of Hanoi, but the Viet Minh lost thousands in a significant French victory.

The Viet Minh persevered despite recurring problems with morale and recruitment. Political officers fought food shortages and the sacrifices required by a seemingly endless war with ongoing indoctrination and propaganda efforts. Hoping to lure French forces away from their strongholds in the Red River delta, the Viet Minh moved into Laos in October 1953.

Many French leaders recognized by then that they faced the dilemma of needing to concede complete independence to counter the nationalist appeal of the Viet Minh, but doing so eliminated most of France's motivation to continue fighting. Victory seemed increasingly unattainable. The French grew increasingly frustrated over American demands that they reject a negotiated settlement while the United States was negotiating to end the war in Korea.

The new French military commander as of May 1953, General **Henri Navarre**, hoped to draw the Viet Minh into a large conventional battle and win a decisive victory. Dien Bien Phu in northwestern Vietnam became the site of that battle. The French occupied the area to prevent Vietnamese infiltration into Laos and support local tribal resistance to the Viet Minh, and established an airfield and strong defensive positions. General Giap surrounded the 13,000 French troops with 50,000 men. Just as importantly, he shocked the French by hauling heavy artillery up the surrounding mountains. The assault began on 13 March, but when human wave attacks proved too costly, Giap switched to digging trenches and tunnels that would slowly squeeze the French defenses. As the French position grew more precarious, US officials debated France's request to provide air attacks. Despite agreement on Indochina's importance to American interests, there was no consensus on the appropriate action. On 4 April President **Dwight Eisenhower** agreed to intervention only if certain preconditions were met: action by an international coalition that would include Great Britain, French consent to Vietnamese independence and continued prosecution of the war, and congressional approval. When these conditions did not materialize, Eisenhower refused to act, and France's requests for outside help went unfulfilled. Dien Bien Phu fell to the Viet Minh on 7 May 1954. The battle cost the Viet Minh 10,000 killed and 15,000 wounded, while French Union forces lost over half of their 15,000 troops, most of whom died as prisoners of war.

The significance of the Viet Minh victory at Dien Bien Phu was magnified by the simultaneous negotiations at the Conference on Far Eastern Problems, which opened in Geneva, Switzerland on 26 April. The Geneva Conference drew participants from Great Britain, the Soviet Union, France, China, the DRV, Cambodia, and Laos. The United States and representatives from Bao Dai's State of Vietnam attended primarily as observers. Designed to find a solution to the political situation in Korea and Indochina, participants turned to Indochinese issues on 8 May, and each had their own objectives and expectations. The DRV assumed its victory at Dien Bien Phu would confer control over all Vietnam, but its representatives achieved significantly less than they expected. America's detached yet menacing presence at Geneva subtly hinted that, should the Viet Minh emerge in control, it might intervene militarily, an outcome that none of the other major powers wanted. Anticipating France's withdrawal, the United States had already begun planning to defend those parts of Indochina not controlled by the Viet Minh from communist expansion. The French used the possibility of US involvement as diplomatic leverage, hoping to retain some influence after their military departure. The Soviet Union had little interest in Indochina at the time and, because the Soviets hoped France would reject a common European defense force, supported limited French goals. Along with the Soviets, the British also favored a political solution. The Chinese, already drained by the Korean War, worried that French war-weariness and impatience with Bao Dai's continued demands for independence might persuade them to turn Indochina over to the United States. China feared escalation in Vietnam, but especially any that involved the United States. Having exhausted themselves in the effort at Dien Bien Phu, the Viet Minh felt unable to improve their position without support and were unwilling to risk American intervention.

With negotiations stalled, new French Premier **Pierre Mendès-France** declared he would resign if unable to end the Indochina war within a month of taking office on 20 June. With France now willing to discuss a partition, the Soviets and Chinese made concessions as well and, less concerned with Vietnamese desires than their own national goals, pressured the Viet Minh to withdraw their military forces from Cambodia and Laos. The Chinese believed these concessions might prevent a failed conference and keep the United States from intervening. The Viet Minh, however, had to defer their ultimate objectives in favor of a bargain the French could accept. The Viet Minh conceded a temporary division of Vietnam, but their major disappointment was in being pressed to accept national unifying elections in two years rather than within the six months they initially demanded.

Participants signed a series of agreements on 21 July that established a cease-fire and temporarily divided Vietnam with a demilitarized zone (DMZ) along the seventeenth parallel. French forces would withdraw into the South while the Viet Minh regrouped in the North. An international commission would monitor the accords and supervise national elections to reunify the country in 1956 [**Doc. 8**]. DRV leaders were frustrated by their less than complete success, but the Chinese and Soviets were more interested in improved relations with the Western powers than in pressing Vietnamese communist goals. The United States, whose hopes for a failed conference had collapsed, did not sign these Geneva Accords to avoid formally recognizing the Chinese government, but agreed to respect them. The French–Indochina War ultimately cost French forces 110,000 dead, while the Viet Minh lost 200,000, with an additional 125,000 Vietnamese civilian casualties (Logevall, 2012: 607, 619).

The United States and Ngo Dinh Diem

Following the Geneva Conference, the Eisenhower administration moved to replace France as the dominant foreign power in Indochina. This was perhaps the crucial decision leading to America's Vietnam War. Concerned that unifying elections would bring Ho Chi Minh to power throughout Vietnam, the United States sought to bypass the Geneva Accords by encouraging a permanent political division that would create a noncommunist state in southern Vietnam. The United States also established the Southeast Asia Treaty Organization (SEATO) combining eight European, Asian, and South Pacific allies to counter communist influence in the region, though Vietnam itself was not a member. The French still hoped to preserve some influence in the South despite their withdrawal, and often clashed with the Americans over policy as long as they retained authority there. Ho Chi Minh established a temporary government in the North, and Bao Dai appointed **Ngo Dinh Diem** as Prime Minister of the State of Vietnam in June 1954. Bao Dai selected Diem largely because of his popularity with several influential Americans, and American support was critical if the State of Vietnam was to survive.

Ngo Dinh Diem had risen quickly through the government bureaucracy to become a provincial governor, and in 1933 he served briefly as minister of the interior in Emperor Bao Dai's government. Although effective in combating communist activity, his outspoken nationalism irritated the French. Diem strongly opposed the social revolution demanded by Ho Chi Minh, favoring a traditional mandarin culture instead. In contesting for power at the end of World War II, the Viet Minh captured Diem, who nearly died of illness in captivity, and buried one of his brothers alive for counter-revolutionary acts. Hoping to broaden his coalition, Ho Chi Minh nevertheless offered Diem the minister of the interior position in his cabinet in February 1946, but Diem refused during a tense encounter. Invited by Bao Dai in 1949 to become premier of the newly formed State of Vietnam, Diem again declined and published a manifesto calling for an alternative to both the French and the Viet Minh. In spring 1950, under a death threat from Ho Chi Minh and denied French protection, Diem left the country. He spent most of the next few years in the United States, where he developed key contacts who would eventually support his political ambitions. With US influence replacing France, "Diem was the only Vietnamese leader who had made himself known in the United States" (Jacobs, 2006: 33).

Nearly one million Vietnamese migrated from North to South during the cease-fire, ten times the number moving North. The US Navy designated this migration Operation Passage to Freedom. While much of migration was deliberate, Colonel **Edward Lansdale** led a clandestine Central Intelligence Agency (CIA) propaganda operation to encourage undecided Northern Vietnamese to relocate to the South. This effort included spreading false rumors about marauding Chinese troops in the North, communist confiscation of private property, and an impending US nuclear attack of the North (Jacobs, 2006: 52–53). This transfer of population, largely comprising Roman Catholics, aided Diem politically, but their arrival created a refugee problem. Initially settled in temporary tent cities, over the next few years they moved into hundreds of new villages that served as enclaves for a religious minority. Diem rewarded them by appointing a disproportionate number of Catholics to key political and military posts. The DRV's influence remained strong in the Mekong delta, however, despite the temporary retrenchment of forces.

Diem faced serious problems in establishing a stable government in the South. After Geneva, the communists focused on building a new government in the North, but thousands of Viet Minh operatives remained in the South after the post-Geneva Accords migration, where they retained control over several southern regions and threatened the new regime. The several Montagnard tribes in the central highlands were ethnically different and both culturally and politically removed from the Vietnamese, who had long viewed them with a degree of condescension and hostility. Diem also faced competition from the Cao Dai and Hoa Hao, religious sects operating primarily in the Mekong delta and Saigon regions, where each exercised local political control. Combined they claimed nearly 3 million adherents and possessed private armies totaling perhaps 35,000 men (Herring, 2014: 63). The Binh Xuyen criminal organization headed by **Bay Vien**, with a militia of 25,000, controlled vice in the Cholon district of Saigon. Moreover, Diem, a Catholic in a predominantly Buddhist society, headed a narrowly based government that featured several members of his own family and ignored representatives from the sects. Noting this limited support and animosity from the French, who retained 160,000 troops in southern Vietnam, some American officials were skeptical of Diem's chances.

General **J. Lawton Collins** went to South Vietnam in November 1954 as President Eisenhower's special representative to assess the situation. With the Vietnamese National Army commanded by political rival General **Nguyen Van Hinh**, Diem lacked a loyal military force. Bay Vien dominated Saigon with his own army, having received control of the national police from Bao Dai in exchange for substantial financial gains. Diem faced public coup threats from Hinh and, despite support in the United States from Senator **Mike Mansfield** and others, his government was critically unstable.

Collins persuaded Hinh to move permanently to Paris, helped reorganize the Vietnamese National Army (VNA), and urged Diem to broaden his government. Nevertheless, Collins advocated backing a new leader, reporting to Secretary of State **John Foster Dulles** that "unless some such action is taken, . . . this country will be lost to communism" (Jacobs, 2006: 68). When the United States shifted its aid from the French directly to South Vietnam, Diem grew more secure in his control of the military. He then moved to end government subsidies to the Binh Xuyen and the religious sects, which then aligned in a "United Front of All Nationalist Forces." On 21 March the United Front demanded that Diem replace his cabinet, but Diem responded by removing police powers from the Binh Xuyen. Bay Vien attacked the VNA headquarters early on 30 March in a bloody but indecisive battle. Later that day, Collins repeated his concerns to Dulles.

With parts of Saigon resembling an armed camp, Eisenhower recalled Collins to Washington to consult with government leaders. Despite some congressional support for Diem, Collins persuaded Eisenhower and Dulles to make a change. On 27 April, Dulles wired orders to the Saigon and Paris embassies to facilitate Diem's removal from the premiership.

Apparently warned of the policy change, within hours Diem attacked the Binh Xuyen forces in a desperate bid to retain power. As the Battle for Saigon erupted, Dulles notified the embassies to delay action on the previous cables. Both the American Congress and the press strongly supported Diem, who surprisingly defeated the Binh Xuyen and drove the religious sects into relative submission as well. By May, he had consolidated his power and regained full US support. France threatened to withdraw its troops if Diem remained in power, but Eisenhower was now committed to him. By backing Diem without insisting on his acceptance of American "standards of performance," Eisenhower limited America's future options. The VNA renamed itself the Army of the Republic of Vietnam (ARVN), and the Americans had effectively replaced the French.

Diem's victory over the sects and the departure of the last French troops in early 1956 doomed the national elections promised at Geneva. Diem further consolidated his power through a blatantly rigged referendum in October 1955 that allowed him to replace Bao Dai as head of state and formally dismantle the monarchy and establish the Republic of Vietnam (RVN). Diem overwhelmingly prevailed, taking over 98 percent of the vote, aided considerably by ballot stuffing, voter intimidation, and campaign restrictions. Diem was not interested in an election against Ho Chi Minh, however, and prominent Americans encouraged him to avoid such a contest.

The Hanoi government soon recognized that its hopes of peaceful reunification and social revolution would be delayed. It was the only Geneva signatory with any real interest in carrying out its provisions, and none of the major powers showed serious inclination to enforce it, nor were they willing to challenge US resistance to holding national elections. Even its benefactor, the Soviet Union, generated little enthusiasm for pressing the Geneva Accords. Hanoi's Prime Minister, **Pham Van Dong**, prophetically told one visitor, "You know as well as I do that there won't be elections" (Duiker, 1981: 172). DRV efforts to carry out the communist revolution also encountered severe problems. Land reforms ultimately provided agricultural land to over half of its population, although zealous revolutionaries executed perhaps 15,000 people and sent thousands more to work in forced labor camps. Ho Chi Minh eventually admitted errors on the part of the government.

Between mid-1954 and the end of 1960, the United States increased its efforts to limit communist influence in Vietnam. American officials hoped to create a viable and permanently separate noncommunist state in the South. In a process it called "nation building," the United States expanded its aid to Diem's government, encouraged economic development, urged social and political reform, and sent advisors for projects such as training a police force. Despite reservations, the United States pinned its hopes on Diem as a nationalist alternative to Ho.

Diem enjoyed significant support from numerous American political leaders, newspaper publishers, and other elites. Many in the press depicted Diem as a "miracle man" successfully blocking the communists in Southeast Asia. Diem visited the United States in May 1957 and received almost universal acclaim. His popularity in the United States, however, far exceeded his popularity in Vietnam.

Diem's actions following the Battle for Saigon did little to broaden his appeal. His rule became increasingly dictatorial and centered on his own family. His brother, Ngo Dinh Nhu became his closest advisor, while his other brothers held powerful religious, military, and diplomatic positions. He dominated the Saigon government and repressed any opposition. The national assembly consisted primarily of members under his control, who approved a constitution he had already prepared.

Diem's excesses lost more support than he gained. His pursuit of political control extended to his personal appointment of provincial and district administrators, and substituting Saigon-appointed village chiefs for local elections. He also alienated ethnic minorities by settling a large, predominantly Catholic population in the central highlands on Montagnard land, and required the commercially vital Chinese population in Saigon to become Vietnamese citizens or forfeit their businesses. The Catholic minority continued to receive inordinate political power and aid subsidies, which the Buddhist majority could not help but notice. Diem's land reform programs failed to redistribute land as effectively as the Viet Minh, and any potential improvements disappeared amid official corruption and incompetence.

To solidify his power, Diem used armed forces to uproot and eradicate the Viet Minh remnants in the South, launching a "Denounce the

Communists" campaign in 1954. His aggressive actions threatened Ho Chi Minh's plans for reunification. Ho had hoped to avoid war and establish a political option to Diem in the South while consolidating his power in the North. Southern communists, supported in Hanoi's Politburo by **Le Duan,** advocated military action against Diem as early as 1956, but the party leadership in Hanoi favored maintaining a political emphasis. Anxious over Diem's growing strength, however, the southerners organized more aggressively against the Saigon regime. Fighting between Saigon's ARVN and southern insurgents broke out in 1957 when Diem sent troops into communist strongholds. Southern party membership dropped from 5,000 to 1,700 that year, as ARVN killed 2,000 and arrested 65,000 suspected communists by the end of 1957. This represented what communists called "the darkest period" of their history (Jacobs, 2006: 90).

Weakened by these attacks, the communist insurgents, now referred to by Diem as the Viet Cong, retaliated with assassinations, killing several hundred local officials of the Saigon government. Skirmishes between small armed units took place in 1958. Le Duan urged a combination of military and political struggle in 1959, and though Ho Chi Minh still hoped Diem's government might fall without force, party leaders in Hanoi accepted the southerners' need to defend themselves more aggressively. Some members of the Politburo were also concerned that without northern support for military escalation, the southern insurgency might grow beyond their control. The first organized shipments of personnel and supplies from North to South began in 1959, often along a primitive infiltration route through Laos that became known as the Ho Chi Minh Trail. Having failed to reach a political solution, Diem's actions had stimulated a civil war. Casualties mounted into thousands on both sides and by 1960 the insurgency threatened Diem's government.

Other problems quickly appeared. Motivated by another rigged election for national assembly members in 1959, several political leaders met at Saigon's Caravelle Hotel and drafted a letter they released to the public on 26 April 1960. This "Caravelle Manifesto" lamented South Vietnam's social conditions, criticized Diem's leadership, and demanded major reforms. Both Diem and the Vietnamese press ignored them.

Recognizing the need to deprive the insurgents of access to the resources of the general population, Diem tried to create allegiance through building **agrovilles** in the summer of 1959. These villages, fortified against infiltration, moved hundreds of families from their ancestral homes to rural areas more isolated from communist influence. Cut off from their traditional lands and forced to build the agrovilles without compensation, peasants generally disliked the program and Diem suspended it in late 1960. Policies like this, combined with Diem's tight family-controlled government, increasingly alienated much of the population. An attempted coup by ARVN units took place in November 1960, but Diem skillfully re-established control. The incident only escalated Diem's efforts to gain the military's loyalty through political promotions. American advisors' counsel for political and economic reform went largely unheeded, and the Eisenhower administration tolerated Diem's despotism.

On 20 December 1960 communists joined with other disaffected groups in forming the National Liberation Front (NLF) to coordinate political matters in the South. Though dominated by communists, the NLF reflected broad support and emphasized national independence over social revolution. Its implementation of land reforms attracted rural support, and, while social pressures and fear pushed some into service, most NLF members joined voluntarily. Hanoi directed the NLF and was now clearly committed to reunifying the country by force if necessary. The war for independence and unification had been delayed by the Geneva Conference, but not ended. As the military component of the struggle, the southern insurgents organized themselves into the People's Liberation Armed Forces (PLAF) early in 1961.

The new American president, **John Kennedy**, expanded the US commitment to Vietnam, viewing the conflict, as did Eisenhower, as communist aggression within the context of the Cold War. A victory by the Vietnamese communists would only encourage, they believed, revolutionary movements elsewhere in the world, and meant an advantage for the Soviets and Chinese. Kennedy's initial Indochina crisis, however, occurred in Laos, where competing factions had lapsed into civil war by 1959. The United States and Soviet Union supplied the opposing forces, but Kennedy temporarily solved his inherited problem when another Geneva meeting re-established a neutral regime in Laos.

In Vietnam, American commitment to Diem increased even as his popular support declined. CIA reports and a Kennedy task force in 1961 both indicated that Diem's political position was deteriorating. With the situation in Saigon reaching a crisis, Kennedy responded by reaffirming US goals of preventing communist victory in Vietnam. Despite public optimism on the part of some American officials, British, French, and Canadian diplomats found American confidence of an early military victory and popular support for Diem misplaced. Despite its reservations, however, the Kennedy administration found the potential alternative of a communist victory intolerable.

Kennedy shifted emphasis toward **counterinsurgency**. Army Special Forces, called Green Berets, trained the ARVN in guerrilla warfare, while the CIA created a local defense program called the Civilian Irregular Defense Groups (CIDGs). Most CIDGs were recruited from mountain tribes, known collectively as **Montagnards**, to provide security and surveillance in the highlands. American officials argued over the best strategy to defeat the guerrillas, but agreed that without more help from the United States the communists would seize control of the South.

In 1962 Diem initiated a new Strategic Hamlets Program designed to fortify existing villages rather than building new ones. The hamlets, surrounded by barbed wire and guarded by military forces, would theoretically isolate NLF guerrillas from potential recruits and other resources. The Saigon government would support their construction and ARVN would defend the hamlets until they were capable of defending themselves. By leaving the villagers in their traditional communities, Diem hoped to avoid the agroville flaws of dislocation and alienation. By the end of the year nearly 3,000 fortified villages existed. In reality, the plan still required a significant percentage of villagers to move, and many were drafted for uncompensated labor. The corruption and failed government promises undermined this program just as they had the agrovilles. Furthermore, as historian Seth Jacobs notes, "once completed, the hamlets were virtual prisons," as villagers faced a regulated daily routine in the name of security (Jacobs, 2006: 127). Regardless, the hamlets proved less secure than hoped. One of the key program administrators turned out to be a communist infiltrator who worked diligently to undermine its effectiveness.

On 15 October 1961 Kennedy sent General **Maxwell Taylor** and **Walt Rostow** to Vietnam to evaluate the potential impact of sending US combat troops into Vietnam. Taylor reported that a crisis existed, but one that could be turned around by increasing American military advisors rather than sending ground troops. Kennedy's leading advisors endorsed Taylor's recommendations, but there was no consensus on whether Diem could implement the social and political reforms that they felt were essential to achieve US goals. On 22 November Kennedy promised an increased effort to block Saigon's fall, known as "Project Beefup," agreeing to provide aircraft, intelligence equipment, and further training for ARVN, as well as additional economic aid.

Diem's refusal to delegate authority and broaden his support by opening up the government to other political factions had long frustrated his American advisors. With family members holding several influential positions, and as part of a Catholic minority, Diem failed to achieve a mass following. Especially troublesome was Diem's brother, **Ngo Dinh Nhu,** who headed South Vietnam's secret police and acted as Diem's closest advisor. The two of them acted in an increasingly oppressive manner. The additional US aid in 1961 and the arrival in February 1962 of General **Paul Harkins** as head of the newly formed Military Assistance Command, Vietnam (MACV) did nothing to change things. MACV coordinated all US military activity in Vietnam and displaced the older Military Assistance Advisory Group. ARVN's hesitancy in attacking the PLAF hindered US war planners, as Diem continued to resist military efforts that might produce significant casualties. One controversial American recommendation was to use herbicides in several areas of the South to remove the cover and food available in the jungle to the PLAF. Several high-ranking Americans claimed progress by the fall of 1962, though advisors such as Lieutenant Colonel **John Paul Vann** believed Saigon's position continued to erode. United States officials in Saigon estimated in September that Diem's government controlled 49 percent of the South, with the NLF holding 9 percent and the rest still being contested. Several Americans doubted the success of the strategic hamlet program. The number of hamlets had expanded more rapidly than ARVN's ability to protect them; they faced NLF infiltration, peasants disliked the control of their lives, and they suffered from Saigon's inefficiency and corruption.

The insurgency grew out of local conditions, but Hanoi provided much of its direction. The Hanoi government viewed Vietnam as a single country and one people temporarily divided by foreign intrusion. Although military confrontations became more frequent, both Hanoi and the NLF continued to emphasize the political struggle for several reasons. They wanted to maintain a low-level conflict to prevent direct US intervention, they still believed that the Saigon government would collapse on its own, and both the Chinese and Soviets wanted to avoid a major military conflict in Southeast Asia. Problems remained, however, as southerners initially contested Hanoi's leadership.

The Saigon government's military situation worsened during 1963. American officials intensified their efforts to have Diem make changes they believed would strengthen his forces, but with no more success than before as popular discontent with Diem continued. One of the first major battles of the war took place on 2 January at Ap Bac, 35 miles from Saigon. Though heavily outnumbered and lacking the artillery and air power of Diem's troops, a PLAF battalion mauled Saigon's forces before retreating at night. ARVN again refused to take the battle's initiative and the regional commander refused to send reinforcements. American newspaper reports of this defeat refuted the optimistic stories that typically came from the Saigon government and American military officials. John Paul Vann's battle report savaged ARVN's performance, but Saigon commanders filed their own versions and claimed victory.

President Kennedy sent Army Chief of Staff General **Earle Wheeler** and Marine Major General **Victor Krulak** to investigate. They criticized the press, complimented Diem's efforts, and returned with a very positive outlook. Other US officials, however, believed that only a strongly nationalistic, noncommunist government that could invigorate the rural Buddhist population had a chance to overcome the NLF. They no longer believed that Diem would ever become that leader. Hanoi was gaining the political edge, though Saigon still held a military advantage. Of 3,700 strategic hamlets, the NLF had destroyed 2,600, and by mid-1963 they controlled a significant portion of South Vietnam's villages and population. By the end of the year the NLF was preparing for an anticipated general offensive and uprising.

Diem's relations with the Buddhist majority in southern Vietnam had been contentious for years, and the conflict finally broke out in open revolt in the summer of 1963. The Buddhist crisis erupted on 8 May when government troops in Hue attacked demonstrators protesting a discriminatory ban on their religious flags and killed several people. Buddhist leaders demanded that the government end its repressive measures against them, but Diem refused to acknowledge the crisis even as demonstrations continued. ARVN soldiers attacked demonstrators in Hue again on 3 June, but under US pressure Diem initiated a truce that the government violated only a day later. On 11 June Buddhist monk **Thich Quang Duc** created an international sensation when he burned himself to death in protest at a Saigon intersection. Press coverage spread photos of the man in flames around the world, and others followed his example. The situation grew worse when Diem's sister-in-law, Madame Nhu, castigated the tragedy as Buddhist "barbecues." The United States insisted that Diem make concessions, and the two sides announced a settlement on 16 June. Rioting the next day in Saigon, however, met with violent repression, and Diem reneged on many of his promises. Diem imposed martial law on 21 August, and midnight raids on Buddhist pagodas throughout the nation by Nhu's police forces resulted in hundreds of arrests and deaths. South Vietnam was on the verge of chaos, but Diem remained obstinate. The Buddhist crisis ended American hopes that Diem would ever establish the political stability essential for success against the NLF.

Concluding that he needed a stronger voice in Saigon, Kennedy appointed the eminent Republican **Henry Cabot Lodge** as the new US ambassador to Vietnam. When Lodge took over on 22 August, ARVN generals informed him of a planned coup against Diem. Though they later backed off, the threat remained. By the end of August, Washington officials were looking for a new government in Saigon that would aggressively pursue the war. Kennedy made several public pronouncements indicating his dissatisfaction with Diem and Nhu. Rumors surfaced that they were willing to make a deal with North Vietnam in order to retain power. A delegation headed by Secretary of Defense **Robert McNamara** and Maxwell Taylor returned in early October with optimism about military possibilities, but with a negative assessment of Diem's political stability. Their evaluation was perceptive as ARVN generals initiated a coup on 1 November and executed both Diem and Nhu the following morning. The Americans had approved of and encouraged the coup, but were shocked by the murders, and struggled to adapt to the new situation.

Diem's removal also brought renewed debate in Hanoi over how to proceed. Ideological divisions were apparent as challenges from General Secretary Le Duan, General **Nguyen Chi Thanh**, and **Le Duc Tho** often prevailed against entrenched decision makers Vo Nguyen Giap, Pham Van Dong, and Ho Chi Minh. The Vietnamese communist leadership decided that southerners should escalate their military and political activity, even though this could antagonize both their Soviet allies and the United States. Ho had often provided the moderate voice in deliberations, but his political rivals no longer felt it necessary to defer to him. In the struggle between the pro-Chinese "South first" faction and the Soviet-leaning "North first" faction, Le Duan pointed to Ho's decisions to disband the ICP and negotiate with the French in 1945, and accept the Geneva Accords in 1954 as ideological errors to undermine his authority and weaken the pro-Soviet wing of the party. Duan's "South first" faction prevailed, created a police state in the North, and sent the first People's Army of Vietnam (PAVN) regiments into the South to prepare for a general offensive in 1964, designed to quickly overthrow the Saigon regime and prevent direct US intervention (Nguyen, 2012: 55–67). During the last decade of his life Ho Chi Minh remained the international face of the Vietnamese revolution, continued as Party chairman, and acted as the nation's senior diplomat and foreign policy advisor. His dominance in Party counsels, however, was over, and his role grew increasingly ceremonial until his death in 1969.

Diem's removal did not resolve South Vietnam's perpetual problems. A long succession of governments, seven in 1964 alone, proved equally incapable of unifying South Vietnam and defeating the communists. Diem was as courageous and as committed to Vietnamese nationalism as his political opponents, but his dictatorial manner eroded his support to the extent that, as historian Seth Jacobs notes, "he steadily reduced his domestic support until, at the end, it barely extended outside his own family" (Jacobs, 2006: 187). Furthermore, none of the Saigon regimes ever completely escaped the taint of colonialism or effectively contested the Viet Minh and their successors as the legitimate heirs of nationalism.

Americans soon encountered an unexpected tragedy that made the challenges of Vietnam even more complicated. President Kennedy was himself the victim of assassination on 22 November 1963. He left to **Lyndon Johnson** a US military force in Vietnam of 16,000 and a commitment to the growing Vietnamese war that was not going well. He avoided, as had Eisenhower before him, making the ultimate decision to leave or commit combat troops. Johnson would not have that luxury.

Johnson's Decisions for War

United States leaders remained committed to Vietnam as a battle in the Cold War. Maintaining their faith in the domino theory, they believed the loss of South Vietnam would threaten other states in the region and endanger America's standing in the world. President Johnson, as had Kennedy before him, also felt that failure in Vietnam would have serious political repercussions from Republicans who had used Democratic presidents in the past as scapegoats for communist advances in Asia. Though Johnson remained committed to Kennedy's policy, he found it necessary to increase US involvement in order to preserve the Saigon regime. He came to realize that there were no easy options. Greatly conflicted over the proper resolution in Vietnam, Johnson believed that taking a stand projected American strength to the communist powers. As historian Robert Schulzinger indicates, "doing more, doing less, or doing the same all entailed enormous risks" (Schulzinger, 1997: 125).

General **Duong Van Minh** served as the new South Vietnamese chief of state, but he proved ineffective in stabilizing the government or fighting the communists. By the end of 1963, Saigon held a substantial edge in manpower and weaponry. The ARVN contained 215,000 troops, plus 83,000 in the civil guard and more than 200,000 irregular forces. The CIA estimated PLAF strength at below 25,000, plus 60,000–80,000 irregulars. Despite this advantage and control of the air, Saigon had not made appreciable gains against the guerrillas. The PLAF increased its attacks and extended its control of areas around Saigon, damaging roads, blocking communication, and collecting taxes. Conditions in the Mekong delta region in particular deteriorated after the coup. US officials noted a decline in military efforts and programs such as the strategic hamlets.

Johnson received conflicting reports about the state of the South Vietnamese government. Few Washington officials felt confident about the new regime. Secretary McNamara and CIA Director **John McCone** both issued pessimistic assessments by the end of the year, with McNamara reporting that without a dramatic change in Saigon's actions, the United States might face a communist victory within three months. Senator Mike Mansfield was among the rare presidential advisors to suggest a change of policy, recommending that a neutral government in Vietnam offered the best hope of avoiding a potentially massive US commitment. National Security Advisor **McGeorge Bundy**, Secretary of State **Dean Rusk**, and McNamara all rejected that view. By January 1964 Johnson's leading military advisors believed that the deteriorated conditions in South Vietnam required a major American effort against North Vietnam.

While US officials discussed how they might influence events, the Vietnamese were making changes themselves. One of Saigon's politically ambitious corps commanders, General **Nguyen Khanh,** led a coup against the government on 29 January 1964. Reactions in both South Vietnam and the United States were mixed, but Washington had already become disenchanted with Minh's weak efforts and hoped Khanh would pursue the war with greater energy. With the proliferation of coups, however, each new regime had to protect itself against political rivals, which drained resources away from fighting the communists.

Despite its early optimism that Khanh would prosecute the war more aggressively, American intelligence indicated continued progress for communist insurgents. At American urging, Khanh had established a two-stage plan for winning the war, first to expand his secure areas near

Saigon and into the southern delta, then to attack and destroy enemy bases. For a conclusive victory, however, US officials, including President Johnson, believed America had to apply military pressure directly against North Vietnam. When the president ordered plans for possible action against the North, the Joint Chiefs of Staff (JCS) recommended covert US attacks against North Vietnamese targets from the air and pressing Saigon to conduct cross-border attacks. Johnson felt that political realities during an election campaign made such moves impractical. The CIA doubted that attacks on the North would improve the situation and could produce serious negative repercussions.

South Vietnam's situation had declined since Diem's death. The National Liberation Front now controlled between 30 and 40 percent of the South and the legitimacy of the Saigon regime had severely eroded. The strategic hamlet program was in disarray, Khanh lacked political skills and failed to take charge of the military. McNamara's visit to Vietnam in March persuaded him that South Vietnam faced a potential collapse. He recommended maintaining an advisory role while expanding the present policy. The United States should build up southern morale by demonstrating its long-term commitment, provide training and equipment so that South Vietnam could increase its armed forces by 50,000 troops, and use American air patrols to block infiltration from Cambodia and Laos. Having rejected withdrawal, neutralization, and attacks against the North, Johnson adopted McNamara's suggestion for its flexibility and because it allowed further delay before having to make more decisive decisions.

The Vietnam debate continued throughout the spring and summer of 1964. Communist military strength had reached the point where they could stand against Saigon forces rather than rely exclusively on guerrilla tactics, but they could not yet hold areas indefinitely against ARVN pressure. US officials debated the effectiveness of air attacks against North Vietnam without reaching a consensus. Johnson's options were not attractive. His advisors wanted escalation but could not guarantee success, while Congress wanted victory at a low cost. "Even with increased US aid," Johnson remarked, "the prospect in South Vietnam is not bright" (Schulzinger, 1997: 144). A May 1964 CIA report reaffirmed Saigon's precarious hold on the population, with the NLF's presence undercutting southern morale. It predicted that if the erosion of Saigon's position did not stop by the end of 1964, "the anti-Communist position in South Vietnam is likely to become untenable" (Schulzinger, 1997: 144). Johnson wanted to avoid communist victory, yet feared a dramatic US escalation would also bring a domestic backlash. The failure of Khanh and his predecessors to fight the war more aggressively produced anger and frustration among some American advisors. The paradox of Americans becoming more influential in Vietnamese life for the purpose of creating an independent state was apparent. They wanted greater control, but believed that for appearances it would be better if Saigon invited them to take over. President Johnson grew increasingly dismayed, telling

McGeorge Bundy at one point, "I don't think it's worth fighting for and I don't think that we can get out. It's just the biggest damned mess that I ever saw . . ." (Woods, 2006: 510).

For several months the Johnson administration considered asking Congress for a resolution giving the president authority to use military force in Vietnam. Johnson worried about the timing, not wanting to disrupt his domestic legislative agenda or draw attention to the war during the election campaign. He also faced critics who opposed military escalation. Finding alternatives to attacking the North as a means of improving Saigon's situation proved difficult. At a meeting on 10 June, advisors argued that a resolution would boost South Vietnamese morale and indicate to both northerners and southerners America's commitment to preserving southern independence. A divided congressional vote would be politically dangerous, so they agreed to wait until North Vietnamese action against the South was clear.

The opportunity for action came within a matter of weeks. American naval vessels had been conducting **DeSoto missions**, electronic intelligence-gathering patrols in the Gulf of Tonkin off North Vietnam. These often took place in conjunction with covert raids by South Vietnamese commandos into North Vietnam, known as **OPLAN 34A** actions. On 2 August North Vietnamese boats attacked the American destroyer *Maddox*, and two days later both the *Maddox* and the *C. Turner Joy* reported being under attack during a night-time storm. Later evidence indicates that this second attack most certainly did not occur. After hearing reports of the alleged 4 August encounter, Johnson ordered US air strikes against North Vietnamese patrol boat bases and an oil storage facility. This encounter provided the desired provocation for introducing a resolution to Congress. McNamara's misleading testimony to the legislators and Rusk's briefing of congressional leaders in the White House persuaded Congress to pass the Gulf of Tonkin Resolution on 7 August [**Doc. 9**]. Only two senators voted against it.

The Gulf of Tonkin Resolution effectively blunted criticism of Johnson's Vietnam policy during the presidential election campaign. **Barry Goldwater,** his conservative Republican opponent, had earlier advocated military escalation, and Johnson managed to portray himself as the candidate of restraint. "We are not about to send American boys nine or ten thousand miles away from home," he told audiences, "to do what Asian boys ought to be doing for themselves" (*Public Papers*, 1965: 155). Having shown his willingness to use force if provoked, Johnson indicated his desire to limit the American commitment. These actions, however, did little to improve the situation for Khanh's government, and despite his best efforts Johnson had not solved the basic problem left to him by Eisenhower and Kennedy.

Plate 1 This young Marine private waits on the beach during a landing at Da Nang, Vietnam. In March 1965, President Lyndon Johnson sent 3,500 Marines to Vietnam, the first US combat troops officially deployed to that country. By the end of the year there were nearly 80,000.

Credit: National Archives and Records Administration (ARC ID 532432).

Plate 2 Soldiers from the US Army's 25th Infantry Division are transported by UH-1D ('Huey') helicopters during a search-and-destroy mission northeast of Cu Chi, Vietnam in May 1966. These large-scale operations were designed to engage and annihilate enemy forces, and deprive them of popular support.

Credit: National Archives and Records Administration (ARC ID 530610).

Plate 3 Elements of the 4th Marine Regiment wade through the water as part of Operation Hastings near Dong Ha, Vietnam in July 1966. This mission attempted to disrupt operations of the People's Army of Vietnam (PAVN) in Quang Tri Province.

Credit: National Archives and Records Administration (ARCC ID 532443).

Plate 4 Meeting in October 1966, these four men played key roles during the Vietnam War: US President Lyndon Johnson, General William Westmoreland, South Vietnamese Lieutenant General (and later President) Nguyen Van Thieu, and Prime Minister Nguyen Cao Ky.

Credit: Lyndon Baines Johnson Library photo by Yoichi R. Okamoto. Serial Number C3598-16.

Plate 5 The Press generally supported the US government's position on the war until after the Tet Offensive, when it reflected the general public's growing disenchantment. Here CBS television anchor Walter Cronkite interviews a Marine commander during the battle for Hue in February 1968.

Credit: National Archives and Records Administration (ARCC ID 532454).

Plate 6 The Army of the Republic of Vietnam (ARVN) was largely trained and equipped by the United States, and fought a significant share of the war with mixed results. These soldiers are with the ARVN 1st Division, November 1969.

Credit: Douglas Pike Photograph Collection, the Vietnam Center and Archive, Texas Tech University, Item number VA002327.

Plate 7 Antiwar sentiment took on various forms, but was extensive and broadly based. These Ohio National Guardsmen use tear gas and advance on student protestors at Kent State university in Ohio on 4 May 1970. Only minutes later the guardsmen opened fire, killing four and wounding nine others.

Credit: 1970 Collection, Kent State University Libraries and Media Services, Department of Special Collections and Archives, image 705/4-1-35.

Plate 8 Marine Staff Sergeant Ermalinda Salazar spent part of her off-duty time working with children at the St. Vincent de Paul Orphanage in Saigon. She was one of nearly 7,500 military women stationed in Southeast Asia during the war, most of whom were medical personnel.

Credit: National Archives and Records Administration (ARCC ID 532499).

Part 2
The Vietnam War

2   America Goes to War

The events of 1964 set the stage for a new phase in the Vietnamese war for independence. By spring 1965 the United States had committed its own troops to direct combat with Vietnamese communist forces. The contest was over the political status of South Vietnam. The United States argued that the war began as northern aggression against a sovereign state in the South, while North Vietnam claimed that American aggression had prohibited the peaceful resolution of the Geneva Accords.

Saigon's Deterioration

The Johnson administration's desire for a limited military commitment was challenged by continued political deterioration within South Vietnam. Nothing disturbed the Americans more than the frequent upheavals within the Saigon government. On 16 August, following the retaliatory strike against North Vietnam, South Vietnamese President **Nguyen Khanh** tried to grab dictatorial powers and undermine his political rivals, but the angry response by street mobs eventually forced him to back down. A September coup attempt failed when blocked by a group of younger American-supported Vietnamese officers, known as the "Young Turks." In October the military leadership installed **Tran Van Huong** as the civilian prime minister, but Khanh, as ARVN commander-in-chief, retained the real power.

By the fall of 1964, the South's internal dissent contributed to the growing strength of the NLF, a situation that the CIA identified as "far more serious than that of November 1963" (Schulzinger, 1997: 158). Viewing the Vietnam conflict as part of the Cold War prevented US foreign policy experts from seriously considering negotiations with the communists or withdrawal from Vietnam. This left a growing, if relatively unenthusiastic, momentum toward greater American military involvement. On 10 September Johnson approved plans proposed by Ambassador Taylor, Secretary McNamara, and JCS Chair Earle Wheeler for a limited escalation designed to strengthen the Saigon government. American ships would continue DeSoto patrols to locate North Vietnamese defenses and radar sites. At the same time South Vietnam sustained its OPLAN 34A operations against the North and increased its military activity near the Laotian border to reduce infiltration of materials down the Ho Chi Minh Trail. Marine and Air Force leaders had argued for a sustained bombing campaign against the North, but Johnson rejected that suggestion.

American efforts seemed to have no impact on stabilizing South Vietnamese politics. Yet another coup attempt in December, this time led by Vice Air Marshal **Nguyen Cao Ky** and General **Nguyen Chanh Thi**, elicited an angry tirade from Ambassador Taylor. Johnson's frustration with the incessant political intrigue was apparent when he exploded to his advisors, "I don't want to hear any more of this coup shit" (*Vietnam: A Television History*, 1996). Khanh's rule had provided no improvement over earlier leaders and failed to unify the South. Buddhist protests again erupted, and political demonstrations became increasingly anti-American.

The succession of coups, recent ARVN defeats at the hands of the PLAF, and infiltration of communist forces into the South reinforced American doubts about South Vietnam's political and military viability. Several high-ranking US advisors believed that South Vietnam's survival as a noncommunist state was in jeopardy. Some feared that Saigon's leaders, in order to preserve their political power, might one day agree to a coalition government unacceptable to American interests, or that the United States would have to assume a significantly larger share of responsibility for South Vietnam's survival.

The Johnson administration struggled to find an effective way to strengthen South Vietnam's political base. A key rationale for limiting US military escalation had been the chronic instability of the Saigon government. American officials, including CIA analysts, believed that actions such as sustained bombing could expose the South to serious domestic disruption, bring a matching response from the NLF and North Vietnam, and possibly induce Chinese intervention. Any or all of these could threaten its existence.

By late November, Johnson's leading advisors moved toward the conclusion that circumstances in South Vietnam required an American bombing campaign against the North. They disagreed, however, on both motive and strategy. Despite intelligence assessments indicating a bombing campaign would have no significant impact on the war in South Vietnam, some advisors argued the bombing would boost southern morale, others that it would reduce infiltration, persuade Hanoi to withdraw its support for southern insurgents, or force them to negotiate. They differed on whether to implement the bombing gradually or introduce an immediate massive attack. Bombing proponents argued that it posed little probability of Soviet or Chinese intervention. Ultimately, one of its greatest attractions was that it appeared less risky than using ground forces.

Although an independent South Vietnam was the US goal, taking this step would increase Saigon's dependence upon America. Political, social, and military instability had left the South in such a vulnerable position, however, that American officials were convinced that the war might be lost if they did not quickly intervene. Johnson agreed that continuing the present policy would lead to defeat.

The notable exception to this emerging consensus was Undersecretary of State **George Ball**. Ball believed that bombing the North would not resolve the South's political instability. He also anticipated that American escalation risked setting in motion a series of events that could force the United States into a long conflict and threaten its control of events.

The lack of attractive options persuaded the administration to adopt bombing as the most promising solution to the existing crisis. On 1 December 1964 Johnson authorized US bombing runs over Laos to harass infiltration efforts, hoping that the implied threat of bombing North Vietnam would encourage Saigon and contribute to its stability.

The North Vietnamese leadership had been divided between those wanting to focus on political development in the North while encouraging political efforts and peaceful unification in the South, and those who favored supporting an armed revolt in the South. By late 1964, Hanoi officials had also concluded that the Saigon regime was near collapse and, wanting to reassure southerners of their commitment, sent the first regular unit of the PAVN into the South at the end of the year. Although anxious about possible American military intervention, recent events suggested that the United States would not dramatically escalate its support of South Vietnam. After the Gulf of Tonkin incident, the United States had absorbed attacks and casualties and watched the South Vietnamese suffer military setbacks without retaliating. A 1 November guerrilla attack on the Bien Hoa air base killed four Americans and damaged several aircraft, and on Christmas Eve insurgents bombed an American officers' quarters in Saigon, killing two and wounding 38. In October the PLAF hit ARVN units in Tay Ninh province on the Cambodian border, and the following month they occupied most of Binh Dinh province on the north-central coast. Two PLAF regiments attacked ARVN outposts near Binh Gia southeast of Saigon from 28 December to 1 January 1965, and held their ground in the face of ARVN counterattacks. Binh Gia showed the communists' ability to fight large battles in a conventional style, and convinced many American advisors that Saigon had lost its military superiority.

American patience ended when the PLAF hit a US military base at Pleiku on 7 February 1965. The attack killed nine soldiers, wounded over 120, and damaged 22 aircraft. President Johnson, using the incident as an excuse to implement previously agreed-upon decisions, ordered an immediate retaliatory bombing strike, known as "Flaming Dart," to hit North Vietnamese military targets just above the seventeenth parallel. A second strike followed an attack on US forces at Qui Nhon three days later. McGeorge Bundy and Assistant Secretary of Defense **John McNaughton**, who had been in Saigon during the Pleiku attack, returned to Washington with a pessimistic report and advocated a sustained bombing campaign against North Vietnam. Bundy claimed that "without new United States action defeat appears inevitable – probably not in a matter of weeks or perhaps even months, but within the next year or so" (*Pentagon Papers*, 1971–72: 3–309).

President Johnson now accepted the conclusion that American intervention provided the only option to South Vietnam's collapse. The argument that Saigon's weakness prohibited escalation had been turned around. As historian George Herring notes, "By the end of January [1965] . . . one of the major arguments against escalation – the weakness of South Vietnam – had become the most compelling argument for it" (Herring, 2014, 156). To save a failing policy, the United States began bombing North Vietnam.

American military escalation required the Soviets to respond in kind if they hoped to contain Chinese influence in Southeast Asia. Under **Nikita Khrushchev**'s policy of peaceful coexistence, the Soviet Union had advised the Vietnamese to avoid provoking a major US intervention. After the Gulf of Tonkin Resolution, however, the Soviets had to substantially increase their military aid to blunt Chinese accusations that they were being too passive. Khrushchev's removal from power in October 1964 facilitated this transition. The Soviets would follow a policy of providing substantial aid to Hanoi while encouraging a negotiated rather than a military settlement of issues and maintaining *détente* as a priority over Vietnamese interests. Soviet aid began arriving in North Vietnam in the first months of 1965, with China permitting Soviet goods to cross its territory by rail. The first Soviet MiG aircraft arrived by the end of May. Soviet aid to Hanoi increased steadily over the next few years, eventually surpassing that of China.

For months the president and his advisors had moved steadily toward a bombing campaign against North Vietnam. Despite the limitations of strategic bombing in World War II and Korea, American Air Force and Navy leaders confidently asserted their ability to weaken North Vietnam's military capabilities and force Hanoi to accept a negotiated settlement with terms favorable to the United States. Other advisors remained unconvinced that bombing would solve South Vietnam's military and political problems, but believed that continuing the present policy ultimately meant defeat. George Ball thought bombing would not succeed, but his was a lone voice. Lacking credible alternatives, the Johnson administration adopted Rolling Thunder as a low cost and politically acceptable measure to achieve its goals.

Rolling Thunder

President Johnson authorized the sustained bombing campaign of North Vietnam, known as Rolling Thunder, on 13 February 1965, and actual bombing runs began on 2 March. The Johnson administration failed to acknowledge that Rolling Thunder represented a fundamental shift in policy from earlier reprisal raids, portraying it as a response to the attack on Pleiku rather than a previously developed plan to overcome Saigon's instability. Pleiku allowed advisors to justify an action that they already favored, but any attack would have worked just as well. The administration rationalized its escalation in a State Department White Paper [**Doc. 10**]. Some US officials expected that Hanoi would concede within six months. Both Congress and public opinion supported the new policy despite some anxiety among a few Democratic leaders.

The administration hoped Rolling Thunder would provide the Saigon government additional time to broaden its political support and assume greater military initiative in the war. McNamara emphasized political goals, anticipating that the threat of increased bombing would intimidate Hanoi into negotiations, and disrupt communications and infiltration into the South. He was also concerned that the bombing would not risk greater intervention by China or the Soviet Union. In line with these views, President Johnson initially kept the bombing away from Hanoi and Haiphong, holding those targets as bargaining chips.

Early raids against the North proved relatively ineffective as US intelligence continued to reveal a deteriorating military situation in South Vietnam. Although Johnson refused to sanction the unrestricted bombing desired by the Joint Chiefs of Staff, he gradually expanded the campaign to include additional targets and more frequent attacks as each level failed to bring the desired results. Bombing in the North ultimately resulted in an estimated 50,000 Vietnamese deaths. Military and congressional critics argued that rather than bomb infiltration routes to achieve a negotiated victory, massive bombing to destroy the North's industrial base would force Hanoi to surrender.

The bombing campaign gave sharp focus to a loose coalition of groups that opposed American involvement in Vietnam. Complaints about US policy had appeared occasionally as the nation's commitment increased in previous months, but Rolling Thunder stimulated larger public actions that would grow into the largest antiwar movement in the nation's history. Among the first actions specifically targeting Vietnam were a series of teach-ins. These college campus-based forums, usually organized by faculty members, generally dissented from military escalation in Vietnam. The first to achieve national attention occurred at the University of Michigan on 24 March 1965. Three thousand people attended a series of lectures and debates that ran all evening and into the next morning. About 120 teach-ins took place on campuses across the country by the end of the spring semester. The largest, held at the University of California at Berkeley, attracted 20,000 participants.

A national teach-in in Washington DC reached 100,000 students by television broadcast. At some universities the war became entwined with other issues such as civil rights, institutional bureaucracy, and leftist politics. Though antiwar activity in 1965 represented a small minority opinion, the early defection of part of the academic community troubled some members of the administration.

Partly in response to critics who argued against military escalation, in a 7 April speech at Johns Hopkins University, President Johnson proposed unconditional negotiations with the North Vietnamese. As an additional incentive he offered a one billion-dollar development program for the Mekong River similar to America's Tennessee Valley Authority. The president was convinced he could persuade the North Vietnamese to bargain on his terms. Johnson had miscalculated. The North Vietnamese responded with four negotiating conditions that demanded US withdrawal and Saigon's acceptance of the NLF program to end the war [**Doc. 11**]. Still hoping for a general offensive and uprising that would topple the Saigon government, Hanoi did not then view peace talks as advantageous to its goals. The United States was no more anxious to negotiate when it expected victory, and it was certainly not inclined to talk under Hanoi's conditions. Neither side was yet willing to compromise on its basic points.

During 1965, the United States and its Vietnamese allies flew sorties against a variety of targets in North Vietnam, but concentrated on military bases and infiltration routes into the South. Johnson implemented a bombing pause from Christmas Eve to the end of January 1966 to encourage negotiations [**Doc. 14**]. American advisors divided over the bombing halt's desirability, with McNamara pushing it and Lodge, MACV commander General **William Westmoreland**, and commander of Pacific operations **Ulysses S. Grant Sharp** opposing it as an opportunity for enemy resupply. The United States hoped that Hanoi would reduce its infiltration of the South as a gesture toward peace talks, but this diplomatic effort did not produce the desired results.

Disappointed with Hanoi's refusal to meet his demands and facing the US military's disapproval, Johnson escalated the bombing, believing that negotiations would eventually come with military victory. Overlooked in the debate was the bombing's failure to stop infiltration or reduce North Vietnam's commitment. When Johnson resumed the bombing, some objections arose from Congress, the media, and antiwar forces.

Unable to find a more viable method of achieving its goals, the United States tripled the number of sorties from 1965 to 1966 as a way to shorten the war and limit American casualties. During 1966 Rolling Thunder expanded to include North Vietnam's oil storage facilities, including those in the Hanoi and Haiphong areas, and destroyed 70 percent of the North's capacity. Sorties reached 108,000 in 1967, dropping 226,000 tons of explosives on North Vietnam. During that year the United States hit electrical, steel, and cement plants, factories, and targets near Hanoi, Haiphong, and the Chinese border with an estimated damage of

$340 million. By the end of 1967 General Wheeler claimed that all important fixed military targets except the northern ports had been hit, and nearly all military and industrial targets in the North were destroyed or damaged. This constituted the most massive strategic bombing in history to that point.

Despite three years of bombing, Rolling Thunder failed to achieve its objectives. Strategic bombing, which is most effective against industrialized nations with mechanized armies, was largely wasted on North Vietnam, a predominantly agricultural society with only a rudimentary industrial base and transportation system. Although the bombing inflicted terrible suffering throughout North Vietnam, it did not significantly limit Hanoi's ability to wage war. Hanoi's army had minimal needs, its industry was not vital to the war effort, and its roads were easily repaired. Increased aid from China and the Soviet Union offset the loss of its own supplies, equipment, and industrial production.

Rolling Thunder had an insignificant impact on infiltration. Northern infiltration of troops into the South actually increased from 35,000 in 1965 to 90,000 in 1967 as Hanoi sent a message that it would match US escalation and continue the war. Northern transport of supplies into the South continued because tens of thousands of Vietnamese worked constantly at repairing roads, railroads, and bridges damaged by bombing. North Vietnam also relied extensively on its waterway system, though Americans countered that by targeting barges and mining rivers. One-third of the North's outside aid arrived by railroad from China, which brought 1,000 tons of supplies daily. China also furnished huge numbers of repair crews and engineers to maintain Vietnam's infrastructure, and their presence near the Chinese border limited US attacks there. Supplies moved south on trucks, railroads, and bicycles, mostly at night to avoid detection.

North Vietnam's air defenses challenged American planes and became increasingly effective over time. The Soviets provided MiG fighters, heavy equipment, and surface-to-air (SAM) missiles, and thousands of technicians for training and operation. Nearly 8,000 anti-aircraft guns served as the main defense, and by the end of 1967 northerners had shot down over 700 US aircraft. Downed pilots made up the largest number of American prisoners of war. The constant ground fire drove other planes off course, making the bombing less accurate. The American air war proved to be very inefficient in another way, costing nearly $10 for every $1 of damage it inflicted upon the North. To reduce Rolling Thunder's impact further, the northern government evacuated many people from the major cities and built bomb shelters all over the country. It also dispersed offices and smaller factories to rural areas. North Vietnam's resolve remained firm [**Doc. 15**].

The air campaign also cost the United States in terms of public opinion. The massive bombing of a small agricultural country disturbed growing numbers of both American and international observers. Despite initial US claims that the bombing hit only military targets, news of civilian casualties reached the public, especially after **Harrison Salisbury**'s reports from Hanoi in December 1966 appeared in the *New York Times*. Even Secretary McNamara ultimately became repelled by the results.

Making the Commitment

The start of the air war led quickly to a dramatic change in the ground war as well. To protect American air bases against anticipated communist retaliation for Rolling Thunder, General Westmoreland asked in late February for American Marines to guard the base at Da Nang. Ambassador Taylor cautioned that introducing US combat troops would cross an important line and could undermine ARVN's incentive to fight, leaving the Americans to carry that burden. Few others, however, saw the move as a turning point. The commitment seemed so small and innocuous that it generated no serious debate.

On 8 March 1965 the first two battalions of Marines splashed ashore at Da Nang. The implications of the move appeared quickly. Before the month was over Westmoreland called for two American Army divisions. The general was concerned over a potential enemy attack and the sluggish South Vietnamese military build-up, and believed that only a significant US combat presence could avoid Saigon's collapse. The Joint Chiefs of Staff enthusiastically supported the request and endorsed offensive operations. Faced with this new warning of Saigon's imminent demise, the Johnson administration again weighed its options.

McNamara met with several high-ranking advisors in Honolulu on 20 April to evaluate American strategy. The group included Ambassador Taylor, Generals Westmoreland and Wheeler, and Admiral Sharp. Westmoreland wanted US troops to take the offensive. With the bombing alone clearly not accomplishing American goals, the group concluded American combat troops were necessary to stave off a southern defeat. They anticipated that a combination of Rolling Thunder and additional ground troops could convince the North Vietnamese that they could not win. Unwilling to withdraw from Vietnam and unimpressed with the results of the bombing campaign, Johnson's advisors saw no better solution. They recommended sending 82,000 additional troops while maintaining the existing level of bombing. Even with this they suggested that it would take at least six months to force North Vietnam to give up its support of the insurgency. By preventing Saigon's imminent collapse, the United States would buy time for the South Vietnamese government to establish military and political control.

Johnson rejected the call for offensive operations, but on 21 April approved deploying 40,000 additional troops to guard US military enclaves. This **enclave strategy** initially limited American troops to operations within a 50-mile radius of their bases. Advocated by Ambassador Taylor as a way of limiting the US military commitment, the defense of enclaves did not have General Westmoreland's enthusiastic support.

Recognizing the possible impact these moves could have at home, Johnson downplayed the importance of his most recent decisions. He carefully avoided a public debate over Vietnam policy, perceiving that anything resembling a declaration of war invited domestic pressures for an unlimited war and could quite conceivably provoke a Soviet or Chinese reaction. He hoped to conduct quietly a low-level conflict without serious congressional oversight. Only in June, and then by mistake, did the administration admit that American troops could take the offensive.

Despite the effort to conceal the war's escalation, segments of the public and government argued for a negotiated settlement to the conflict in Indochina. The international community also criticized America's new direction in Vietnam, and the United States received little support from its traditional allies. United Nations Secretary General **U Thant** and Canadian Prime Minister **Lester Pearson** were among the foreign leaders who publicly disapproved of the bombing campaign.

Johnson did, in fact, make some effort to open negotiations. In addition to his Johns Hopkins speech, he initiated a five-day bombing pause over North Vietnam in early May to probe Hanoi's eagerness for mutual de-escalation, although this effort was largely to appease the war's critics rather than a serious attempt to negotiate. The administration's primary goal continued to be an independent South Vietnam, a situation that the North Vietnamese and NLF found unacceptable. North Vietnam responded to the bombing pause with its own negotiating demands, which the president rejected. When Johnson requested $700 million in May for the war in Vietnam, members of Congress knew he saw the vote as a test of their support for his policies, even though most legislators found those policies to be vaguely defined. With the commitment already made and soldiers in the field, Congress had little choice but to approve even had members been inclined to question events in Vietnam.

President Johnson pressed America's Pacific allies to commit soldiers to South Vietnam's defense. South Korea sent 60,000 troops and Australia 8,000, but other nations such as New Zealand, Thailand, the Philippines, and Taiwan provided more modest contributions. Non-Vietnamese allied forces peaked at 71,000 in 1969, but the United States carried the major burden after 1965.

As the summer progressed, it became increasingly clear that America's latest efforts to reverse the war's fortunes were not succeeding. Westmoreland's reliance upon US troops did little to enhance ARVN's desire, confidence, or abilities. While occasionally used in conjunction with American forces during field operations, ARVN was generally relegated to a secondary role with responsibilities in the unpopular **pacification** programs that emphasized village security. The United States continued to provide training throughout this period, but in the American style, which kept ARVN increasingly dependent upon the United States. By late May, continuing problems with morale and desertion, plus recent defeats at the hands of PLAF and North Vietnamese troops induced within ARVN an attitude that the war should be left to the Americans. A turbulent political situation accompanied the South's military problems. Military leaders led by Air Marshal Nguyen Cao Ky and General **Nguyen Van Thieu** shunted aside **Phan Huy Quat**'s civilian government in June. Ky assumed the premier's position while Thieu took control of the military.

Despite their reservations about the competence of the new government, American military officials argued for an intensified bombing campaign of the North. Westmoreland and the JCS also continued to push for a significant increase in US ground troops and a shift to an offensive strategy. The escalation of guerrilla activity and continued poor performance by South Vietnamese troops led Westmoreland to request in June an additional 150,000 US troops. He and the Joint Chiefs of Staff had never supported the enclave strategy, and now JCS Chair Earle Wheeler argued, "You must carry the fight to the enemy. No one ever won a battle sitting on his ass" (Graff, 1970: 128). Secretary McNamara traveled to Vietnam to assess the situation and returned in agreement with Westmoreland. In early July he recommended 100,000 additional troops and congressional approval to call up the reserves. Notably, McNamara's proposal did not promise victory, only to "stave off defeat in the short run and offer a good chance of producing a favorable settlement in the longer run" (Johnson, 1971: 145).

The president's advisors again supported military escalation, with the exceptions of George Ball and unofficial counselor **Clark Clifford**. Ball doubted whether Americans could win in Vietnam, and argued that a dramatic escalation could produce a "protracted war involving an open-ended commitment of US forces, mounting US casualties, no assurances of a satisfactory solution, and a serious danger of escalation at the end of the road" [**Doc. 12**].

McNamara's pessimistic report and his carefully constructed choices left the president with no apparent option but to escalate [**Doc. 13**]. At the end of July, Johnson increased bombing runs in both North and South Vietnam, though he withheld approval for an unrestricted bombing campaign of the North for fear of Chinese intervention. He also granted an immediate addition of 50,000 troops for Vietnam, agreed to 50,000 more by the end of the year, and implied that additional troops would be available if needed. Furthermore, Johnson authorized the use of American troops in independent military actions. With this commitment of additional ground troops, the bombing campaign's primary rationale became interdiction and weakening the North's war-making ability rather than breaking Hanoi's will. The president was abandoning the enclave strategy, and this open-ended commitment would guide his policy until the end of his term.

These July decisions transferred the burden of fighting from the South Vietnamese to the United States. Even at this juncture, the credibility of America's international commitments played a key role in Johnson's decision. Yet the president's policy of gradual escalation was the same failed approach tried earlier. The Saigon regime was no stronger and the NLF no weaker than before. What was different, though he tried to hide it from the public, was that the United States had assumed a dramatically increased role in military operations.

Ironically, throughout these discussions of how to ensure an independent South Vietnam, the Vietnamese themselves were not consulted. Americans made the decisions, informed Saigon's leaders, and expected their assent. "The Americans came in like bulldozers," Ambassador Bui Diem later remarked, "and the South Vietnamese followed their lead without a word of dissent . . ." (Bui Diem, 1987: 153).

Both military and civilian advisors urged Johnson to inform the public and secure its support for this significant change in policy. Johnson, however, still believed that acknowledging a shift to an American-dominated war risked retaliation from China and the Soviet Union and threatened his domestic agenda, then making its way through Congress. His announcement on 28 July denied that it represented a change in policy and deliberately hid its significance. Despite his decision, Johnson seemingly remained unconvinced that Americans could win under the circumstances that existed in Vietnam. George Ball held the same view, and argued that the new policy offered little promise of victory. Ball believed this was the last chance to avoid a commitment that would cost thousands of American lives and limit the nation's ability to extricate itself. Even Ball, however, acknowledged the perils of cutting America's commitment in 1965, and he did not offer a concrete proposal for doing so. As the only consistent opponent of escalation, he failed to persuade the president, though his warnings ultimately proved remarkably accurate.

By the summer of 1965, most senior government officials involved with Vietnam had already arrived at what they believed to be the only viable solution to their dilemma. Few were willing or able to look at Vietnam from a new perspective. They also believed that the United States would succeed, and saw failure to achieve their goals as having serious implications for the credibility of America's foreign policy. This limited range of options would take the nation into a major tragedy. They agreed that doubling the number of US combat troops could prevent communist victory without stimulating a domestic backlash. In rejecting the call-up of reserves, they hoped to portray the move as a continuation rather than a break with past policy. This deception would later cause Johnson credibility problems of his own. Most members of Congress, informed rather than consulted, publicly supported the shift, though many were uneasy with its implications.

Ultimately the Americans' fear of the consequences of a communist victory overcame their reservations. Though he did everything possible to deny it, Johnson's July decisions represented America's declaration of war, though certainly not through constitutional channels. This seemingly offered the least painful course to avoid defeat and of avoiding the undesirable measures of withdrawal or total war. Johnson heard, but did not accept the arguments of either Ball or the Joint Chiefs of Staff. The flaw in Johnson's plan was that there was no indication of what level of force would be sufficient to produce an acceptable negotiated settlement, and how the public would respond. "Miscalculating the costs that the United States would incur," notes George Herring, "the administration could not help but overestimate the willingness of the nation to pay" (Herring, 2014: 175).

The Ground War

Having committed their military power, the Johnson administration assumed with a supreme confidence that North Vietnam could not long stand against them. Lieutenant **Philip Caputo,** one of the first combat Marines to serve in Vietnam, remembered that "we carried, along with our packs and rifles, the implicit convictions that the Viet Cong would be quickly beaten and that we were doing something altogether noble and good" (Caputo, 1977: xiv).

The United States believed it could preserve a noncommunist South by forcing North Vietnam to withdraw its support for the southern insurgency. Johnson wanted to escalate American force levels until it reached North Vietnam's breaking point, exhibiting the administration's determination to Hanoi, yet showing restraint to minimize Chinese and Soviet intervention. Gradual escalation, however, often antagonized US military officials who felt it gave the North time to adjust to American strategy.

The Americanization of the war increased US troop levels from 23,000 at the end of 1964 to 385,000 during 1966, and 535,000 by early 1968. Americans poured into Vietnam prepared for a conventional war that emphasized large unit engagements, but the PLAF and North Vietnamese often utilized guerrilla warfare. There were no clearly marked front lines. Communist forces usually selected the time and place to engage ARVN and US units, permitting them to control their own losses as they attempted to wear down the Americans over time.

Unlike the air war, President Johnson gave General Westmoreland great flexibility in designing and conducting ground operations.

Westmoreland's strategy of **attrition** focused on the US Army's traditional doctrine, which emphasized firepower and mobility. Initially he moved to secure the heavily populated coastal areas and break the enemy's momentum. During this first phase he developed the logistical base necessary to support a larger force. Westmoreland believed he could then end Saigon's military deterioration by the end of 1965 and regain the initiative by attacking the NLF in their mountain bases and blocking infiltration from the North. During this second phase he hoped to impose a conventional war upon the guerrillas, which held distinct advantages for the United States. As the number of American troops steadily increased, Westmoreland expanded the use of what were popularly called **search and destroy** operations to find and eliminate the communists' larger regular units and base camps. By targeting remote areas, they could use their tremendous firepower without endangering heavily populated areas. The Americans relied on attrition to wear the enemy down and force them to negotiate a settlement favorable to the United States. With that accomplished, the Saigon government would be strong enough to control the South without American support. Westmoreland initially believed he could stop the insurgency within 18 months.

American military leaders relied upon superior technology to gain an advantage over communist guerrillas. The United States established "firebases" of artillery to support ground patrols on search and destroy missions. Air attacks often provided support for infantry operations as well. More than two-thirds of the bombs dropped during the war fell on the South, targeting enemy strongholds, supply routes, and supporting villages. Helicopters provided air mobility for transporting troops, but the guerrillas were more mobile on the ground and maintained closer contact with the peasants in the battle for hearts and minds. The United States used herbicides to destroy jungle foliage and crops that might provide cover or food for the NLF. Under Operation Ranch Hand, the United States sprayed over 3.6 million acres in Vietnam from 1964 to 1971. Agent Orange was the most widely used defoliant, and as early as 1969 scientists linked that chemical to health problems.

Critics of the search and destroy strategy claimed that it left the communists in control of the countryside and permitted the PLAF to determine the circumstances of military contact. Counterinsurgency experts argued for protecting populated areas to deny guerrillas access to the people. Westmoreland, however, continued to rely on technology and firepower. One American officer typified the US resistance to pacification when he remarked, "That's not the American way and you are not going to get the American soldier to fight that way" (Krepinevich, 1986: 170).

Pacification concerned the political, military, and economic security of Vietnamese citizens. It included activities as varied as training and leading village defense units, establishing schools, implementing land reforms, and organizing elections. The United States did make modest efforts in pacification. The Marines, responsible for the northern provinces of South Vietnam, committed more resources to pacification than did the Army. As early as 1965 some Marines operated in combined action platoons (CAPS), composed of a US rifle squad and a corpsman, plus a Vietnamese Popular Forces platoon. The CAPS stayed in specific villages for extended periods of time, providing security and military training, conducting night patrols and ambushes, and developing intelligence. At its peak the CAPS program operated in over one hundred villages and built an impressive record. These attempts, however, were limited, never involving more than a few thousand troops, and were often undercut by the attrition strategy. Bombing and village sweeps brought fear and destruction to rural areas, producing the loss of valuable rice production and millions of refugees who typically lived in crowded conditions on urban fringes.

The US military measured its progress in this war of attrition by counting the number of casualties. This "body count" proved an unreliable measure given the difficulties in achieving an accurate battlefield tally and in differentiating between combatants and civilians. Americans often echoed Philip Caputo's rule of thumb, "If it's dead and Vietnamese, it's VC" (Caputo, 1977: xix). The military chain of command in Vietnam also encouraged exaggerated counts, as higher numbers often brought military promotion, and US officers later acknowledged inflated figures. One of the assumptions of the attrition strategy was that the United States would eventually eliminate more enemy soldiers than could be replaced, called the **crossover point**. Once the communists hit the crossover point and found their available forces reduced, they would be forced to capitulate. With 200,000 North Vietnamese reaching draft age each year, however, and with the enemy largely determining its own casualty rate, their losses always remained within acceptable limits. Nevertheless, PLAF and North Vietnamese forces suffered heavy casualties by the end of 1967, estimated by the Americans to be as high as 220,000. On this basis, military and civilian leaders claimed that the United States was winning.

Hanoi recognized by the end of the summer of 1965 that the increase in US troops and China's reluctance to promise additional aid to the Vietnamese meant the delay of an anticipated general offensive and uprising in the South. Each side now believed it had no choice but to escalate militarily to match the opposition.

North Vietnam responded to the American challenge, determined to outlast them by waging a protracted war, much as they had done against the French. As Premier Pham Van Dong observed, "Americans do not like long, inconclusive wars . . . thus we are sure to win in the end" (Van Dyke, 1972: 30). To win a protracted war, however, the communists needed the continued protection of southern peasants. While Americans postponed political activity and pacification, Hanoi and the NLF emphasized the connection between the political and military struggles.

North Vietnam matched US escalation through recruitment in the South and increased infiltration of personnel and equipment down the Ho Chi Minh Trail. The trip usually lasted from two to six months. Between 10 and 20 percent of those making the journey succumbed along the way to illness, accident, or bombing. For a time Hanoi moved supplies down the coast, but US naval patrols eventually limited that route's effectiveness. They had greater success shipping through the Cambodian port of Sihanoukville and moving overland to South Vietnam. The Cambodians tolerated this to avoid problems with Hanoi. President Johnson blocked strong military action to keep from pushing neutral Cambodia into the communist camp.

On the battlefield, North Vietnamese troops initially concentrated their attacks on ARVN and avoided US forces unless they enjoyed favorable circumstances. During 1966, however, General Nguyen Chi Thanh, commander of the **Central Office for South Vietnam (COSVN)** from 1965 to 1967, matched US escalation and pursued a more aggressive strategy. The resulting increase in casualties from the People's Army of Vietnam's units drew criticism from General Giap, among others, as too costly and risky.

Early search and destroy operations against the insurgents gave US military leaders some cause for optimism. The Marines' August 1965 Operation Starlite in Quang Tri province produced a favorable kill ratio of over 13–1. When American forces returned to their base camp, however, the NLF regrouped and re-established its dominance in the area, a cycle repeated in several regions for the war's duration.

The first major engagement between American and North Vietnamese regular forces took place near the Ia Drang River valley. On 19 October a PAVN regiment attacked the Plei Me Special Forces camp located in west-central South Vietnam. A second regiment laid an ambush for any relief units coming from Pleiku. The US 1st Cavalry division aided ARVN in breaking through to Plei Me on 26 October as the battered PAVN forces withdrew to the Ia Drang valley near the Chu Pong mountains.

On 27 October Westmoreland ordered the 1st Cavalry to find and destroy PAVN units in the area. The major contact came on 14 November when the nearly 450 men of the 1st battalion unknowingly landed by helicopter in the vicinity of 2,700 PAVN troops. Within a few hours the battle of Ia Drang was under way, and as most of the battalion defended the landing zone, one American platoon was cut off and surrounded. The PAVN attacked early on 15 November, but the reinforced Americans withstood the assault and rescued the stranded platoon. Heavy artillery shelling and B-52 strikes caused one PAVN regiment to withdraw, and a final attack on 16 November failed. The United States estimated more than 1,200 communist casualties.

After airlifting the 1st battalion out on 16 November, two other battalions continued the operation. One of those fell into an ambush on the following day and the PAVN moved as close to the American positions as possible to minimize their vulnerability to US air and artillery fire. When American reinforcements fought through, the PAVN units withdrew during the morning of 18 November. This action cost the United States 151 dead. The operation ended on 26 November without further significant contact.

The battle of Ia Drang provided lessons for both sides. To the Americans it seemingly validated the attrition strategy. United States forces had blunted the PAVN's effort to cut the South in half through the heavy application of firepower and air mobility. American artillery fired over 33,000 rounds and, with B-52s and close air support, had helped prevent the infantry from being overrun and forced the communists to withdraw. The entire five-week operation cost the PAVN 3,561 men while the United States lost 305. Ia Drang also marked the first mass use of helicopters to transport troops into battle, which became standard American practice during the war. The North Vietnamese learned to ignore the lure of search and destroy missions and avoid direct confrontations with US troops. When they did engage large American units, they minimized US firepower by moving as close to their perimeter as possible. They called this "clinging to the belt." General Giap, who opposed matching the Americans in a conventional war, called for greater emphasis on guerrilla tactics and sought to tie down US forces in the highlands. Ultimately he hoped to make the war too costly for the Americans.

Ia Drang might also have given both sides reason to pause. Hanoi may have been prepared to make great sacrifices to achieve national unity and independence, but the costs indicated by this early test would be enormous. The Americans' apparent success offered the false promise of a military solution to the Vietnamese conflict, and they consequently gave little attention to pacification. Recognizing that communist escalation was exceeding his own, Westmoreland requested at least 25,000 more troops. McNamara visited Saigon in late November and again returned to Washington with a pessimistic report.

Lingering concerns within the military about US strategy reemerged in the wake of this engagement. In the spring of 1965, US Army Chief of Staff General **Harold Johnson** initiated a study of American strategy in Vietnam, completed in March 1966 as the "Program for the Pacification and Long-Term Development of South Vietnam" (PROVN). The study suggested emphasizing village level security for the civilian population and uprooting the Viet Cong infrastructure over the existing search and destroy operations. PROVN had its advocates, but Westmoreland and the Joint Chiefs of Staff generally dismissed its arguments and disregarded its recommendations. The basic ideas, however, would gain favor later.

By mid-1966 Westmoreland had established an extensive support base, and his allied forces enjoyed a 4–1 numerical advantage. Communist forces also lacked adequate heavy weapons or air power. Starting at the end of the year, US and South Vietnamese forces undertook several major offensives against enemy base camps. United States officials reasoned that these areas were critical enough to the PAVN and PLAF war effort that they would be forced to defend them, giving the Americans the conventional battles they preferred. The search and destroy operations that took place in 1966 and 1967 inflicted significant casualties and cost the enemy valuable supplies, but did not seriously affect their ability to continue fighting. When faced with unacceptable losses, the communists could control their casualty rates simply by retreating underground and waiting for better conditions.

Operation Attleboro took place from 14 September to 24 November 1966 in War Zone C northwest of Saigon. Planned to locate communist base camps and force a fight, the major contact took place in November. A PLAF division faced a combined US and ARVN force that reached 22,000 men. The communists suffered over 3,000 casualties along with the destruction of a key base camp. American and South Vietnamese losses totaled 650. Attleboro represented another successful use of air mobility and firepower. In six months, however, the PLAF had returned.

In January 1967 Westmoreland followed up with Operation Cedar Falls. It targeted an area 20 miles northwest of Saigon known as the Iron Triangle, long dominated by the NLF. The goal was to destroy the NLF infrastructure by using hammer and anvil tactics; dropping a blocking force in the field by helicopter and using a second force to drive the communists into the first unit. On 8 January US forces attacked and evacuated the village of Ben Suc to remove civilians and create a free fire zone. They then unleashed an artillery and aerial bombardment followed by an infantry sweep. The Americans leveled the villages and surrounding jungle vegetation before engineers used explosives to wreck nearly 12 miles of underground tunnels. They concluded by burning the area to eliminate cover for the guerrillas and a bombing assault to weaken or destroy the remaining tunnel complexes. Two US and one ARVN division were involved in the 18-day operation. The NLF lost 750 killed and over 800 prisoners or defectors, while allied forces suffered almost 430 killed and wounded. The main enemy force, however, avoided confrontation and returned in strength within months. Civilian refugees created by the operation became more hostile to Saigon than before.

Operation Cedar Falls reveals the inherent limitations of the American strategy. Despite its firepower and military superiority, the operation achieved only partial success. It certainly created real problems for Hanoi and the NLF, in some instances producing morale problems and a decline in popular support. As the war escalated, recruitment became harder and conscription and taxation by the NLF increased. At the same time, however, American strategy wasted resources and antagonized the civilian population.

Operation Junction City followed soon after, hitting War Zone C and targeting the 9th PLAF division. It began on 22 February with 22 US and four ARVN battalions, the largest operation of the war to that point. United States units blocked the area on three sides while additional forces advanced from the south. The heaviest fighting took place in late March, though the operation continued until 14 May. American forces utilized close air and artillery support to fight off PLAF assaults. United States and ARVN casualties included 282 killed and 1,576 wounded, and the communists lost over 2,700 killed. The direct threat to their base camps caused the communists to move the Central Office for South Vietnam across the border to Cambodia. Although bloodied by the attack, the 9th PLAF division returned to join the Tet Offensive the following year. As one US general remarked, "It was a sheer physical impossibility to keep the enemy from slipping away whenever he wished if he were in terrain with which he was familiar . . ." (Krepinevich, 1986: 191).

These major search and destroy missions allowed the Americans and South Vietnamese to inflict high casualties and disrupt communist operations, but they did not destroy enemy units or deprive them of those areas beyond the time of the operation. The war still consisted mainly of small unit engagements, and the PLAF and PAVN initiated about 90 percent of all military encounters.

By the end of 1967 America's attrition strategy had failed to meet its objectives. United States military escalation had prevented an apparent defeat, but achieved no quick and painless victory, only a stalemate. Despite significant losses and a huge discrepancy in military power, Hanoi continued to thrive. From 1965 to 1967, the communists sustained an estimated 179,000 combat deaths compared with 13,500 American and 40,000 South Vietnamese. During the same period, however, the communist troop level in the South increased by 42,000 as they matched each US escalation and avoided the crossover point. By emphasizing the body count, the United States failed to gain control of territory that would deny the enemy its support. "While the Army killed many VC," Andrew Krepinevich concludes, "it never denied the enemy his source of strength – access to the people" (Krepinevich, 1986: 197). The lack of pacification meant that Americans fought the same units for the same territory numerous times after "destroying" them. Search and destroy also worked to the advantage of the North's protracted war strategy. They drew the US forces into remote areas for inconclusive battles. With nearly 450,000 US troops in Vietnam, Westmoreland still anticipated years of war.

Although large unit engagements usually favored the Americans, the American style of war also presented problems. Unexploded ordnance provided the guerrillas with explosives, while extensive bombing interfered with Vietnamese farming and caused significant civilian dislocation and casualties. The flood of refugees and migration to the cities further disrupted an already unstable society. One US official in the Civilian Operations and Revolutionary Development Support (CORDS) program compared efforts to achieve American objectives with "trying to build a house with a bulldozer and a wrecking crane" (Thompson, 1977: 225).

The American escalation did prevent the collapse of the South Vietnamese government, but the war continued. Northern infiltration into the South proceeded and the enemy felt no compulsion to negotiate for peace. Unwilling or unable to alter its mission to fit the Indochinese situation, American reliance on technology did reduce US casualties, but failed to achieve the hoped-for military and political goals. Vietnamese persistence ultimately proved the greater weapon.

Given this assumption that overwhelming military power would carry the day, America's civilian and military leaders never devised an appropriate strategy for victory. The failure of the initial commitment brought succeeding increases in troop levels that also failed. The predictions of a half-million troops that had been ridiculed as absurd in 1965 turned into tragic reality. By 1967, after over two years of the American war effort, conditions had changed very little. The assumptions that military efforts could achieve political stability in Saigon and that limited war could achieve victory quickly enough to prevent domestic unrest both proved to be incorrect. Combined with a gross underestimation of the enemy's resourcefulness and commitment, it was a plan for failure. If civilian leaders established limits for the war's conduct, however, they left strategy to the armed forces. American military commanders failed to adjust to either civilian restraints or the specific circumstances of Indochina. Their pursuit of a conventional war in very unconventional circumstances also made victory significantly more difficult to achieve.

Turmoil in the South

The situation in South Vietnam gave no indications of improvement, and US intervention was crucial to the South's survival. The military regime headed by Ky and Thieu since June 1965 did provide some stability. Their rivalries and distrust of one another, however, precluded effective administration of either the war or the government. Their policies were often as repressive as Diem's had been. The heart of South Vietnam's political instability was the lack of a popular, broadly based government in Saigon.

Political tension erupted following a Honolulu summit meeting on 7 February 1966. United States officials once again pressed Premier Ky to implement reforms. Ky announced that the ruling military "Directory" would draft a constitution and turn the government over to civilian leadership within a year. Buddhist monks, students, and other dissenting groups, however, responded to Ky's rigid control by resuming public protests, beginning in Hue and Da Nang, but spreading quickly to Saigon and beyond. This "Struggle Movement" resented the military's ties to the Americans and many of the protests contained obvious anti-American sentiment as well. The demonstrators advocated democratic elections, social reforms, and a civilian-controlled government, and some called for an end to foreign intervention, demands which Secretary of State Dean Rusk found "unrealistic."

The crisis worsened when troops in Hue and Da Nang supported the dissidents. When the government attempted to suppress the protests with armed force, Ky and Thieu clashed with General Nguyen Chanh Thi over putting down the revolt in Da Nang, and fired him as I Corps commander in March. This only inflamed the protesters who demanded that Ky and Thieu resign. The United States supported the government's military efforts to end the unrest, fearing that new leadership would negotiate with the enemy. In mid-May, Ky ordered South Vietnamese troops to take control of Da Nang, and rebel forces withdrew. On 19 May ARVN attacked the Buddhist pagodas, and South Vietnamese units fought each other in those cities for several weeks. Opposition continued in several cities into June when Saigon forces ended the last effective resistance. Though the government successfully suppressed the dissidents and emerged with greater power than ever, the political costs were high and the underlying problems remained. The military rank and file, by religion and politics, were often distant from their commanders.

The Buddhist crisis helped drive the progress of the Revolutionary Development Program. This cooperative venture between the Americans and South Vietnamese sent teams into villages to live and work with the peasants to build support for the Saigon government. These Revolutionary Development (RD) teams struggled with a lack of adequate manpower, funding, and training, as well as bureaucratic inefficiency, suspicious local officials, and occasionally ARVN misbehavior. The inability to provide security to the villagers undermined pacification programs. The US military paid little attention to these efforts, while ARVN was either unable to do so or was itself a security problem. The lack of coordination between pacification and offensive operations meant that US planes occasionally bombed the very villages that Revolutionary Development was trying to protect. The RD teams were also frequent targets of PLAF attacks. The first year's results provided only minimal gains, and during 1967 the program was given to the US Military Command.

Westmoreland convinced ARVN to emphasize securing the countryside, and in the long run they did achieve somewhat better results.

Although the South Vietnamese government ratified a new constitution in April and held national elections in September as part of its promised reforms, South Vietnam did not evolve into a true democracy. Elections to the National Assembly were tightly controlled, and the executive branch maintained the authority to assume dictatorial power in an emergency. The government successfully maneuvered to limit opposition candidates and was generally supported by Ambassador Henry Cabot Lodge (*Pentagon Papers*, 1971–72: 2–384). In the ongoing struggle for power, Ky was forced to exchange positions on the ticket with Thieu, but even with their manipulations and rigid control, Thieu and Ky won with a plurality of only 35 percent of the vote. The second-place finisher, with 17 percent, advocated negotiations with the NLF. While some claimed the vote provided respectability for the regime, others saw it as symbolic of Saigon's weakness.

The Thieu regime imprisoned and even tortured political opponents, and its police force's political surveillance surpassed that of Diem. Corruption remained a serious problem within the Saigon government. The ARVN faced ongoing morale problems. The majority of young men resisted serving, and the army lost one-third of its soldiers each year to desertion.

Southerners, both military and civilian, often saw the war as the Americans' war. With US forces in Vietnam, their incentive to fight was dramatically reduced. American tactics contributed to Vietnam's domestic problems. The Vietnamese often resented the Americans for the bombing, defoliation, and the creation of refugees who poured into the cities and overtaxed their resources. The American presence drastically changed Vietnamese culture as the South grew increasingly dependent upon the United States.

Americans and South Vietnamese developed a pervasive mutual distrust. US troops from top to bottom displayed little faith in ARVN's military abilities. Infiltration by the NLF into South Vietnamese armed forces created a fear of security leaks that caused Americans to withhold key military information from their allies. US resentment of these allies rose with the number of American casualties. They found it difficult to differentiate between friends and enemies. If southern peasants could avoid the mines that routinely killed GIs, Americans concluded, they must be the enemy. Trusting Vietnamese villagers became nearly impossible when any peasant could be a guerrilla.

Likewise, the Vietnamese viewed the Americans with suspicion. Peasants had to balance the benefits provided by the Americans with their frequently rough treatment and a condescending attitude. The overwhelming US presence in Vietnam seemed to some as no better than a foreign occupation.

The war's impact spread far beyond the battlefield into every corner of Vietnamese life. Perhaps the most tragic was the flood of refugees, estimated at four million South Vietnamese, or 25 percent of the population. Torn from their native villages, they either poured into the already overcrowded cities or jammed into squalid refugee camps. Not surprisingly, the experience of being uprooted from their traditional homes left many southerners angry and potential recruits for the NLF.

The rapid arrival of a half-million US troops and the billions of dollars that poured into Vietnam seriously disrupted an already unstable society. Bars and brothels sprang up around military bases. The infusion of American goods and money drove prices sharply upward and broke down traditional family and economic relationships. A flood of US consumer goods severely damaged South Vietnam's own industries and made the country even more dependent upon the United States. Much of the southern population made its living working for the Americans.

Corruption spread on a scale unprecedented in Vietnamese society. Government workers often required bribes for their services, and both Americans and Vietnamese cooperated to make money on a lucrative black market. These activities eroded US efforts to strengthen the South Vietnamese economy. Though some American officials pressured the Saigon government to weed out corrupt officials, the virtual guarantee of continued US support at that time gave them reduced political influence. Other Americans saw corruption as less important than other issues or feared that stronger action might make the political situation even worse.

Certainly, the cultural gap between Americans and Vietnamese made the entire effort more difficult. The political attempt to build a strong, broadly based government in Saigon was no more successful than the military effort to destroy the NLF and North Vietnamese. The survival of the Thieu regime was based primarily upon US military strength rather than popular support.

Given this unsatisfactory military and political progress, the rapid rise of popular discontent in the United States was not surprising. Both organized dissent and passive public opinion indicated a growing disaffection with the war. By early 1968 American policy in Vietnam had reached a crisis point both at home and abroad.

3   Turning Points

The war's escalation raised serious questions and produced a growing debate in the United States over the desirability of the American commitment. "Hawks" urged a stronger and more aggressive military strategy to win on the battlefield, while "doves" argued that the war violated American interests and values. The eruption of the Tet Offensive in early 1968 caused many in both the government and general public to re-evaluate the country's relationship to the war in Vietnam. The ensuing debate brought a change in US policy and increasingly bitter divisions in American society. Americans were fighting the war at home.

The Antiwar Movement

American military escalation in 1965 produced an immediate and organized public opposition. As the months passed, it grew dramatically, becoming one of the largest social movements in the nation's history. Ultimately, as part of a larger period of social unrest, antiwar forces contributed to a general questioning of America's direction and values, and produced a national anxiety that limited the government's options in prosecuting the war.

The anti-Vietnam War movement grew out of existing peace and social justice organizations involved in civil rights or anti-nuclear activities. Mass demonstrations, typically organized by broad coalitions of national and local groups, attracted the greatest publicity, but most antiwar efforts took place at the local level. Political liberals made up the movement's largest constituency, initially through groups such as the American Friends Service Committee, the Committee for a Sane Nuclear Policy (SANE), and Women Strike for Peace. While their motives for opposing the war varied, liberals were generally proud of America's record in advancing human rights, and accepted Cold War suspicions of the Soviet Union. They believed, however, that Vietnam drained resources from more important foreign interests and objected to supporting Saigon's authoritarian regimes. They used education, electoral politics, and peaceful protest in calling for a negotiated settlement in Vietnam rather than continued fighting.

Pacifists, divided into liberal and radical camps, had long disputed America's Cold War policy. Their international perspective assigned equal blame to the United States and the USSR for global instability. Pacifists often overlapped with liberals in their views and memberships, but organizations such as the Fellowship of Reconciliation and the Committee for Nonviolent Action were predominantly pacifist. Liberal pacifists favored electoral efforts, political lobbying, and direct action to change what they saw as a misguided policy. Radicals perceived fundamental flaws in American society of which Vietnam was only a symptom. They viewed electoral politics as nonproductive and often used nonviolent civil disobedience to protest US actions.

Leftists remained a minority within the antiwar coalition, but played an increasingly visible role as the war continued. The small faction-ridden Old Left operated through political groups such as the Communist and Socialist Workers' parties. They fought each other as hard as they attacked the capitalists. Despite their radical critique of American society, they favored legal and peaceful demonstrations, and demanded immediate US withdrawal from Vietnam. More influential was a growing New Left, a student-oriented movement that rejected both Marxist dogma and capitalist inequalities. The New Left's main outlet, Students for a Democratic Society (SDS), began as a liberal reform organization, but as the 1960s progressed its national leadership became increasingly radical and advocated violent tactics. The leadership went so far left that it abandoned most of its local membership, which remained predominantly reformist.

Given the wide diversity of the antiwar constituency, disputes over goals and tactics were not surprising. Two issues proved particularly divisive. Liberals distrusted communist motives and feared association with them would damage their credibility with the public. As a result, they sought to exclude communists from antiwar demonstrations. Pacifists argued for the broadest possible coalition and that democracies should support the rights of all political tendencies. Most mass demonstrations followed a nonexclusionary policy. The second issue was over the preferred solution to getting out of Vietnam. Liberals favored negotiating with the North Vietnamese over a mutually acceptable settlement. Radicals argued that only the Vietnamese had the right to determine their future and that the United States should withdraw its troops immediately.

Despite accusations from government officials and conservatives that antiwar forces were communist-controlled, the movement was clearly indigenous and too broad and loosely organized to be manipulated by any single element [**Doc. 16**]. The movement was a constantly shifting coalition that attracted, or repelled, activists depending upon events in Vietnam and at home.

The Rolling Thunder bombing campaign had stimulated a wave of teach-ins across the country. Local antiwar actions continued until the war's conclusion. The public's awareness of the movement came primarily through the media's coverage of mass demonstrations. Throughout the war the various antiwar tendencies organized coalitions to stage these events. The first was the National Coordinating Committee to End the War in Vietnam (NCC), which sponsored the international days of protest in mid-October 1965. The movement's internal tensions were evident when the NCC refused to back a separate antiwar rally on 28 November because its sponsor, SANE, excluded communists. The NCC faded away over factional disputes, but local groups such as New York's Fifth Avenue Peace Parade Committee carried on the commitment.

As SDS shifted focus to broader reform issues and withdrew from antiwar leadership, liberals and pacifists dominated activity during 1966–1967. Hearings by the Senate Foreign Relations Committee in February 1966 raised new questions from respected quarters about America's role in Vietnam. Chaired by Senator **J. William Fulbright** (D-AR), the nationally televised hearings forced the Johnson administration to defend publicly the rationale and details of its policies. Based on this debate, most of the committee members endorsed a negotiated settlement. Later that year, the war occasionally appeared as an issue in the fall elections. Antiwar activity escalated during 1967 as new organizations formed or older ones shifted their focus to ending the war. Greater numbers of people unaffiliated with organized political and social groups attended demonstrations as frustration with the war grew.

Martin Luther King Jr. joined the public debate against the war in early 1967. In speeches delivered in February and April, King declared that "the promises of the Great Society have been shot down on the battlefields of Vietnam" and referred to the US government as "the greatest purveyor of violence in the world today" (Hall, 1990: 41–42). His position as the most respected civil rights activist in the nation brought added weight to antiwar arguments, though some believed he would compromise civil rights gains by speaking against Johnson's policy in Vietnam. Few national civil rights leaders or government officials welcomed his voice against the war. Accusations of communist affiliation followed to undercut the movement's influence, though the vast majority of antiwar activists rejected Marxist ideology.

A new national coalition, the Spring Mobilization Committee to End the War in Vietnam, sponsored rallies in New York and San Francisco that brought liberals, radicals, and pacifists together. The inclusion of communists, however, eventually kept some liberal organizations away. Nevertheless, the 15 April demonstrations were among the largest yet: 200,000 in New York and 50,000 in San Francisco.

While the leadership of the national coalitions fought continually over tactics and ideology, most activists were unaware or unconcerned with those debates. Their actions in local communities and attendance at national rallies were directed toward ending the war. Activists tended to be middle class and well educated, and college students made up a significant portion of the crowds. While mass rallies encouraged antiwar activists and offered alternatives to existing policy, they did not by themselves change the war's direction. Most Americans in 1967 were not willing to pull out and accept a defeat in Vietnam.

Liberal antiwar efforts in the summer of 1967 included Negotiation Now!, which placed advertisements and petitions in major newspapers to support congressional doves. It proposed a bombing halt and general cease-fire. Another was Vietnam Summer, designed to inform citizens of the war's impact across the country in door-to-door efforts. Vietnam Summer fell short of its hopes, however, meeting apathy or hostility in working-class and poorer neighborhoods.

The military draft was among the most divisive issues during the war, and stimulated a great deal of antiwar activity. The Selective Service System allowed conscientious objection, though it was not easy to obtain, and a system of deferments and exemptions favored the middle and upper socioeconomic classes. Antiwar activists established draft counseling centers to educate men about their options in dealing with the system. Tens of thousands resisted the draft through both legal and illegal methods. On 16 October 1967 an organized antidraft group called The Resistance collected over 1,100 draft cards from men who refused induction, a federal crime. In Oakland, police fought street battles with 3,500 radicals attempting to close down the Oakland Army Induction Center. Resistance to the draft, whether organized or conducted individually, concerned the government, which tried to punish antiwar activity by withdrawing exemptions from activists.

Draft resistance was part of a larger trend within the movement. Many of those who felt legal protest had proven ineffective in changing US policy shifted to direct action, what they called going "from protest to resistance." More people also found connections between the war and their daily lives. In Madison, Wisconsin, for example, students attempted to block recruiters from Dow Chemical, makers of napalm, and faced a police attack for their trouble.

The antiwar actions of the fall culminated with the 21 October 1967 March on the Pentagon. Nearly 100,000 people attended a Washington DC rally at the Lincoln Memorial, with speakers calling for a bombing halt, a negotiated settlement, and US withdrawal from Vietnam. Half of the demonstrators marched to the Pentagon for a two-day confrontation that brought over 600 arrests and focused national attention on the country's disintegrating consensus. Despite the presence of violent elements, the frustrated majority of the movement remained committed to peaceful change.

Although public support for the war gradually eroded, antiwar activists never achieved widespread popularity. The presence of countercultural clothing and hairstyles, plus radicals' display of North Vietnamese flags and anti-American rhetoric at antiwar protests antagonized many moderates. The government's deliberate and misleading attacks on the movement added further to its negative image.

The Debate in Washington

Disagreements about the war's progress also surfaced within the government itself. By mid-1967 the Vietnam War had moved painfully to a stalemate, a situation that favored the North Vietnamese strategy of a protracted guerrilla war. In spring, Westmoreland and the Joint Chiefs of Staff called for 200,000 additional troops, a limited mobilization of the reserves, and authorization to conduct operations into Laos, Cambodia, and North Vietnam. Despite general agreement that the air war had failed, they also called for more bombing of Hanoi and Haiphong, as well as the mining of Haiphong harbor. At the same time, civilian advisors were abandoning existing policy. George Ball and Press Secretary **Bill Moyers** had resigned in 1966. Robert McNamara had turned against the war and proposed transferring greater responsibility to Saigon. He also favored a halt to the bombing to encourage negotiations. CIA reports questioned military claims of US success. Following South Vietnam's October 1967 elections, Vice-President **Hubert Humphrey** was publicly optimistic, but privately he commented, "America is throwing lives and money down a corrupt rat hole" (*U.S. Government*, 1994: 895).

President Johnson was troubled by the lack of progress, but skeptical of the military's belief that higher troop levels would make a difference. For political and military reasons he also found a shift in the bombing campaign unacceptable. That did not imply, however, a willingness to abandon the American commitment. Johnson granted an increase of 55,000 troops and expanded the target list for Rolling Thunder, though more out of frustration than any belief that these would improve South Vietnam's military or political situation. In September 1967 the president proposed a modified negotiating position called the "San Antonio Formula." Assuming the enemy would not escalate its infiltration, he offered to stop the bombing of North Vietnam in exchange for productive discussions. For the first time he agreed to consider the NLF's political participation.

To assess his policy, Johnson convened an informal group of 16 advisors known as the **Wise Men** on 1–2 November. This unofficial body of several former government leaders all opposed withdrawal and largely supported the existing policy. They suggested, however, a less costly ground strategy and a greater use of South Vietnamese troops to deter the erosion of public support that came with open-ended but indecisive fighting.

Although there were some indications that the situation was improving in Vietnam, domestic support for the war was in serious decline. American officials viewed the situation with grave concern. The administration tried to mobilize greater support for the war with a barrage of optimistic reports. The president brought General Westmoreland and Ambassador **Ellsworth Bunker** back to the United States in November as part of a public relations campaign to persuade Americans that things were going well. Johnson grew increasingly frustrated with dovish critics and tried to undercut them through surveillance and harassment.

The Tet Offensive

At the end of January 1968, PLAF and PAVN troops launched their most massive attack yet during Tet, the lunar new year and Vietnam's most important holiday. Known as the Tet Offensive, it proved to be a tactical defeat for the communists, but ultimately achieved an enormous political victory.

The concept of a general offensive and uprising had guided North Vietnam's strategy since the early 1960s. Believing that the existing stalemate offered potentially significant gains, in July 1967 Le Duan's faction presented plans for a massive conventional military assault during the 1968 Tet holiday. Moderates such as Ho Chi Minh and Vo Nguyen Giap believed this approach was unsound and favored negotiations. Duan rejected serious negotiations without a military advantage, outmaneuvered his opponents, and purged many of the moderates. With Le Duan having prevailed in a bitter power struggle, both Giap and Ho temporarily left the country as planning for the offensive moved forward (Nguyen, 2012: 101–109).

Scholars disagree on what motivated the Tet Offensive. Some argue that northerners were worried about mounting losses and pursued a conventional assault as a desperate measure to stay in the war. Most, however, believe that Hanoi remained optimistic about its ultimate success. Le Duan believed the offensive could stimulate a popular uprising and the formation of a coalition government. A few might have looked for the collapse of Thieu's regime and maybe even an American withdrawal. A majority more likely expected a less decisive change, such as a halt to the bombing or a weakened government in Saigon, and viewed the offensive as part of a long-term strategy of "fighting while negotiating."

Hanoi planners intended to lure US troops into the countryside with diversionary attacks against remote outposts. These targeted the areas south of the demilitarized zone (DMZ) separating Vietnam's two sections and along South Vietnam's western border. This would make the cities more vulnerable. At the same time North Vietnam prepared to initiate new attempts to negotiate with the United States. While negotiating, the PLAF and PAVN would launch simultaneous attacks against the South's major cities, which had previously been relatively insulated from the fighting. The communists hoped these actions would spark a popular uprising [Doc. 17].

In October and November of 1967 Hanoi's new plan went into effect when the PAVN attacked a few isolated villages and bases in the South's central highlands. The Americans initially responded as the North Vietnamese had hoped. Interpreting the moves as an effort to gain control of the northern provinces, General Westmoreland sent troops into the countryside, driving back PAVN attacks at Con Thien, Loc Ninh, Song Be, and Dak To, and inflicting heavy losses. In the meantime, NLF forces began infiltrating into urban areas. Southern insurgents attempted to broaden the popular front against the Saigon regime, utilizing political favors and propaganda to create a wedge between Washington and Saigon. To antagonize the Saigon government, in December Hanoi announced its willingness to negotiate with the United States if it stopped bombing the North.

The focal point of these diversionary attacks came when two PAVN divisions laid siege to the Marine base at Khe Sanh in northwestern South Vietnam on 21 January 1968. Falling for the North's strategy completely, some American leaders believed Khe Sanh represented Hanoi's attempt to achieve another Dien Bien Phu, and President Johnson called for its preservation at all costs. Westmoreland sent 6,000 troops to reinforce the defenders, and American B-52s led aerial assaults that pounded the enemy with one of the heaviest bombings in history, over 100,000 tons on a five-square-mile area.

With the United States focused on Khe Sanh, the second stage of the offensive was set for the beginning of Tet. Since Tet typically brought a mutual cease-fire, Hanoi assumed that the South Vietnamese would be relaxed and unprepared for an assault. Just after midnight on 30 January 1968, 84,000 PLAF and PAVN soldiers attacked most of the significant urban areas across the South, including 36 of 44 provincial capitals, 64 district capitals, and five of the six major cities. In Saigon, 20 guerrillas broke into the US embassy compound, and others hit the presidential palace, the Tan Son Nhut airport, and the South Vietnamese general staff headquarters.

The Tet Offensive achieved almost complete surprise. US intelligence had gathered some information of infiltration into southern population centers and captured documents that outlined the general plan. American commanders, however, were so convinced that Khe Sanh was the real target and that the enemy was incapable of conducting an offensive on such a massive scale that it viewed the captured documents as a diversionary tactic. "Even had I known exactly what was to take place,"

Westmoreland's intelligence officer later conceded, "it was so prepos-terous that I probably would have been unable to sell it to anybody" (Westmoreland, 1976: 421).

Despite catching the Americans and South Vietnamese by surprise, communist forces were not as well coordinated as they might have been. The intense secrecy of the planning allowed very little prepara-tion time, and the recent purges robbed Hanoi forces of some valuable military leadership. Some premature attacks gave the United States time to reinforce weak areas. The rapid response permitted little time for the attacking forces to establish solid defensive positions, and they received disappointingly little help from the civilian population. ARVN fought more effectively than most Americans had expected. South Vietnamese and US troops inflicted heavy casualties and took many prisoners, driving the PLAF out of most cities within a few days.

The worst fighting took place in Hue, where 7,500 PLAF and PAVN troops overran the older section of the city known as the Citadel. It took over three weeks for US and South Vietnamese forces to expel the com-munists, who suffered nearly 5,000 casualties. Bombs and artillery shells left the city in ruins, and the fighting created 100,000 new refugees. While in control of Hue, communists executed nearly 3,000 civilians, whom they considered to be supporters of the Saigon government, and buried them in mass graves. Two thousand more disappeared.

Tet did not bring about the collapse of South Vietnam, as Hanoi dis-covered a lack of revolutionary fervor in Saigon. Communist forces sus-tained probably 30,000 dead and wounded, though American estimates ranged as high as 40,000. Westmoreland's perception that Tet cost the communists dearly was accurate. The NLF, which suffered the greatest losses, never completely recovered from Tet. It was badly crippled as a fighting force and its political organization was seriously damaged, although it remained operationally effective. Two smaller offensives later that year yielded similar results. Le Duan's failed strategy caused North Vietnam to revert to Giap's protracted war during one of the revolu-tionary movement's most challenging periods. Growing dissension in the North led Le Duan to impose even greater repression to maintain power.

The communists did achieve some success, however. As ARVN forces moved into the cities for defense, they created additional problems for a Saigon regime already facing serious urban problems. Tet also under-mined South Vietnamese pacification efforts. With many rural areas now abandoned, thousands of villages and hamlets returned to NLF control, some for the first time since 1965.

The Americans suffered over 1,100 casualties, ARVN lost 2,300, and another 12,500 civilians were killed. The offensive created an estimated one million Vietnamese refugees. By late spring and summer, the United States and ARVN regained much of the territory lost during Tet. Recog-nizing limits to their commitment, however, American officials had by then chosen a new approach. Through Tet, North Vietnam had broken the pattern of American escalation.

For much of the American public, the Tet Offensive was a rude awakening to the realities of the war that prompted a re-evaluation of the nation's commitment. Having been repeatedly told by leading political and military leaders that the communists were fading and that there was light at the end of the tunnel, the public was stunned to find them still capable of such an effort. Pictures of close-quarter fighting appeared on their television screens and in newspapers and magazines, reminding them once again of the ongoing human costs of the war. The new reality reinforced public discontent with the war.

The press reflected the American public's response to Tet and interpreted the offensive as a psychological blow to the US effort. Having generally accepted the optimistic reports of government authorities, they found the continued claims of victory far less credible. Respected television newscaster **Walter Cronkite**'s reaction epitomized the media's shock when he exclaimed, "What the hell is going on? I thought we were winning the war" (Oberdorfer, 1971: 158). The reality of the offensive clashed with the optimistic reports of recent months, and Johnson's credibility plummeted. Public opinion polls showed a drop in support for Johnson's conduct of the war. In this light many people re-evaluated the motivations for being there. The senseless destruction was epitomized in the words of an American officer who helped drive the enemy from the village of Ben Tre, "It became necessary to destroy the town to save it" (Oberdorfer, 1971: 184). While General Westmoreland remained optimistic, other US intelligence reports offered a more negative assessment. Government officials were shocked by Tet and remained unsure whether the communists would follow with another offensive. Others continued to believe Khe Sanh remained the primary enemy objective.

The battle for Khe Sanh continued for a few days beyond the end of the Tet Offensive. Massive American firepower eventually drove the North Vietnamese back. In June, however, only weeks after lifting the siege, the United States abandoned Khe Sanh for a more secure, mobile base. To walk away from a site that so recently had been proclaimed a vital position further strained the president's credibility with the public and emphasized the war's irrationality.

For General Giap, the Tet Offensive vindicated North Vietnam's protracted war strategy. Speaking of the Americans, he claimed, "Until Tet they had thought they could win the war, but now they knew that they could not" (Macdonald, 1993: 269).

The Nation Reconsiders

General Westmoreland and the Joint Chiefs of Staff hoped to use the Tet Offensive as a rationale to mobilize the nation's military reserves. They planned to use these additional troops to expand the war into North Vietnam, Laos, and Cambodia, as well as strengthen America's global commitments in the wake of recent Cold War flare-ups in Korea and Berlin. At a late February meeting in Saigon, Wheeler persuaded Westmoreland to ask for 206,000 additional troops, half of which would be sent to Vietnam by the end of 1968. Wheeler returned to Washington from Saigon and reported pessimistically that Tet had been "a very near thing," with defeat in some areas blocked only by rapid US reinforcements. He predicted a renewed communist offensive and contended that more troops were necessary unless the United States was "prepared to accept some reverses" (Turley, 1986: 616–617). Wheeler was less convinced than Westmoreland that the enemy was vulnerable, but he crafted his comments to gain the president's approval for reinforcements. Rather than achieve their purposes, Wheeler and Westmoreland opened Vietnam policy to a major re-evaluation.

Faced once more with unappealing choices, President Johnson asked incoming Secretary of Defense Clark Clifford to evaluate Westmoreland's troop request and "Give me the lesser of evils" (Johnson, 1971: 392). Since his May 1965 dissent from sending combat troops, Clifford had consistently supported the president's policy in Vietnam. His new appointment, however, prompted him to ask again the fundamental questions in order to provide a reliable evaluation. His civilian advisors examined the implications of more escalation, as well as possible alternatives, and concluded that the existing policy had failed (*Pentagon Papers*, 1971–72: 4–558). Clifford's discussions with military leaders led him to believe that additional troops offered no guarantee of greater success and would require greater costs and commitment from the American people than they seemed willing to provide. Further, they could not predict when South Vietnam could successfully resist communist forces independently and offered no new ideas for success. As Clifford later related, "Nothing had prepared me for the weakness of the military's case" (Clifford, 1991: 494). The secretary's advisors recommended moving from search and destroy to a strategy of population security, but advocated only a token troop increase.

The Tet-induced debate of Vietnam policy brought the opposing factions into sharp focus. Westmoreland and Wheeler attacked the Defense Department proposal and defended their more aggressive strategy of cross-border pursuit and occupation of limited areas of North Vietnam. The Joint Chiefs of Staff also favored sending more troops. Clifford had shifted to supporting de-escalation, and recommended that Johnson reject the military request, but did not suggest a change in overall strategy. He also proposed a cessation of bombing over North Vietnam to encourage negotiations. Secretary of State Dean Rusk echoed Clifford by recommending bombing limitations and increased efforts to negotiate with Hanoi.

Although Johnson remained publicly optimistic, he questioned the long-term effectiveness of the existing policy. He was deeply troubled at the prospect of giving up in an area where a long-standing commitment had been made. Johnson convened the Wise Men again in late March, but a majority surprisingly concluded that de-escalation should begin immediately. Most agreed that America's goal of an independent non-communist South Vietnam was probably beyond its grasp. The president found their conclusions deeply disheartening.

President Johnson rejected Westmoreland's request to expand the war. The stabilization of the Tet crisis, the consensus of his leading advisors, public opinion, and a March economic emergency all contributed to his decision. With no apparent need for significant reinforcements, Johnson sent only 13,500 additional troops. He also brought Westmoreland back to the United States to become the Army's Chief of Staff. General **Creighton Abrams** replaced him, taking charge of MACV on 3 July 1968. The president had moved toward ending military escalation and contemplated a bombing halt and new peace efforts to resolve the war diplomatically.

In the wake of Tet the American media took an increasingly unfavorable view of US policy. The early misperception that Tet was a North Vietnamese military success went largely unchallenged. Both print and television media questioned America's commitment, perhaps best summarized in Walter Cronkite's 27 February broadcast:

> To say that we are closer to victory today is to believe, in the face of the evidence, the optimists who have been wrong in the past. To suggest that we are on the edge of defeat is to yield to unreasonable pessimism. To say that we are mired in stalemate seems the only reasonable, yet unsatisfactory conclusion.
>
> [Doc. 18]

When the *New York Times* broke the story that Westmoreland had requested 206,000 more troops, more public protests followed. Despite criticism from Westmoreland and others that a hostile media turned the public against the war, numerous studies refute this charge.

Congress reacted as well. The Senate Foreign Relations Committee conducted hearings on the war on 11–12 March, and the following week members of the House of Representatives called for a complete review of Vietnam policy. These responses reinforced the Johnson administration's belief that additional escalation would prove increasingly divisive.

Public opinion polls indicated a growing lack of confidence in the president's handling of the war. Public disaffection found a political outlet in Senator **Eugene McCarthy**'s challenge for the Democratic presidential nomination. Running largely unnoticed as the year began, his campaign received a significant boost from the Tet Offensive. His strong support in the New Hampshire primary also enticed **Robert Kennedy** to enter the race as an antiwar candidate.

In a 31 March television speech, President Johnson announced that bombing in North Vietnam would be restricted to just north of the demilitarized zone, and called for North Vietnamese military restraint and a willingness to negotiate. He concluded with the shocking announcement that he would not run for re-election [**Doc. 19**]. This speech ended America's escalation in Vietnam, though Johnson still hoped to achieve the nation's long-standing goals. His biggest fear was the collapsing home front. The president's change of tactics promised no improvements to the existing situation.

Negotiations

Although President Johnson had shifted tactics, he had not deviated from his original goals. He agreed to negotiate with Hanoi, but still refused to compromise on fundamental issues. On the battlefield, American troops applied continuing pressure against the communists. None of these efforts, however, succeeded in breaking the military stalemate. Some of the president's key advisors, including Rusk, Bunker, and Walt Rostow, an assistant for national security affairs, agreed with military officials that Tet had badly hurt the enemy, which made concessions at the negotiating table unnecessary. Other officials, such as Clifford and **Averell Harriman**, concluded that the war was a disaster that interfered with more important global issues, and pressured Johnson to de-escalate. The two factions fought bitterly over control of the president's policy. Clifford remembered, "The pressure grew so intense that at times I felt the government itself might come apart at its seams" (Clifford, 1991: 476).

Johnson's offer to negotiate, though evidently sincere, was accompanied by serious doubts that Hanoi would accept. Le Duan in particular distrusted diplomatic solutions. The losses incurred during Tet, however, plus their desire to stop the bombing gave northern leaders incentive to open talks. They also viewed negotiations as part of a new offensive that they hoped would drive the South and the Americans apart and encourage dissent within the United States. Within days of Johnson's 31 March speech, Hanoi accepted talks regarding the bombing. While the quick and positive response caught the administration off guard, it had to accept.

The two sides ultimately agreed upon Paris as an acceptable site for preliminary discussions, and talks began on 13 May. Johnson initially maintained an uncompromising position, which virtually guaranteed that little would happen. Hanoi was similarly not inclined to enter serious negotiations while its military forces were on the defensive. For them the Paris talks initially offered a political opportunity, and they insisted on a complete halt to bombing before further discussions could take place. Johnson would stop the bombing only if the North also de-escalated. The lack of progress brought increased pressure from the military to escalate once again. Averell Harriman, Johnson's chief negotiator, urged a complete cessation of bombing over the North and recognition of reduced combat in Vietnam as the North's informal acceptance of US demands. Johnson resisted this advice and publicly warned of renewed escalation if the talks proved unproductive.

To improve its position in Vietnam, the United States increased military operations during the spring of 1968, especially from the air. B-52 missions tripled during 1968. United States and South Vietnamese forces jointly conducted the war's biggest search and destroy operation during March and April, using over 100,000 troops in the Saigon area. Although General Abrams reduced the scale of American operations later in the year, he maintained heavy pressure on communist troops. His command in Vietnam, however, implemented significant revisions to the ground war. Reflecting the 1966 PROVN study that largely repudiated search and destroy, Abrams pursued a clear and hold strategy that combined conventional operations with pacification. Both US forces and ARVN gave greater priority to population security over wearing down PAVN and NLF military units to control as much of the countryside as possible. At the same time Abrams hoped to improve ARVN capabilities and disrupt enemy logistics. Saigon increased the size of its local forces and supplied them with better equipment. This Accelerated Pacification Campaign produced only superficial improvements rather than sustained effective security. Scholars disagree about the assessments of post-Tet pacification efforts, but the most persuasive study argues that progress was almost solely the result of US forces and disappeared with their departure. Historian Kevin Boylan concludes that "the insurgency survived, the GVN [Government of Vietnam] failed to win the active support of the rural population, and **Vietnamization** did not succeed" (Boylan, 2016: 270). The Chieu Hoi and Phoenix programs attempted to encourage defections from the enemy and inflict damage on the NLF's infrastructure. Not until the end of 1968, however, did pacification efforts reach their pre-Tet levels, and greater village security did not necessarily translate into political support from the peasants.

The United States also began to shift a larger share of the fighting to the South Vietnamese, what **Richard Nixon** would later call Vietnamization. American officials readily admitted, however, that the Saigon government was not yet capable of defending itself. South Vietnam would enlarge the size of its military forces and receive better equipment and training, then would gradually assume a larger responsibility for the war. General Abrams increasingly used US and South Vietnamese forces in combined missions. Despite efforts to improve ARVN, problems of desertion and leadership remained, and most US officials remained unimpressed with its performance. Having followed the Americans for so long, many Vietnamese were unenthusiastic about Vietnamization.

The United States did identify political improvements in Saigon's effectiveness, especially in rebuilding the cities after Tet. The government, however, still rested upon a narrow political base. It failed to implement land reform in a timely manner or deal effectively with the growing refugee problem. The start of negotiations and the possibility of US withdrawal made Thieu even less willing to share power, and drove South Vietnam's political factions further apart. Many South Vietnamese, in fact, opposed negotiations, fearing that a settlement would mean an American withdrawal that would leave them exposed to the NLF.

The Tet Offensive produced noticeable effects upon the NLF and PAVN. Americans observed a decline in the quality of communist units and defections from northern forces increased. Their efforts to rebuild their organizations often alienated villagers. They remained, however, an effective military force and launched significant attacks in the South during May and August; 1968 proved to be the war's bloodiest year.

Back in the United States, domestic clashes increased during 1968, many of them motivated by differences over America's role in Vietnam. On several occasions civilian authorities called out military troops to deal with the unrest. Two national leaders, Martin Luther King Jr. and Robert Kennedy, were assassinated. At the Democratic national convention that year in Chicago, it appeared to many that "the war in Southeast Asia . . . was causing a kind of civil war in the United States" (Zaroulis, 1984: 200).

The issue of a halt to bombing played an influential role in that fall's presidential race. Democratic nominee Hubert Humphrey trailed Republican Richard Nixon by a significant margin until, on 30 September, he publicly broke from Johnson's Vietnam policy and endorsed a cessation of bombing over North Vietnam to encourage negotiations. From that point on Humphrey gained momentum, though Johnson was offended by what he saw as his vice-president's betrayal. By delaying any offer of ending the bombing linked to negotiations, the president may well have cost Humphrey the election. Not until 31 October did Johnson stop the bombing over North Vietnam after the military assured him that it would not threaten the US position.

Encouraged by the Soviet Union, Hanoi agreed to resume talks within four days of a halt to the bombing. The United States and North Vietnam dealt with the delicate problem of political recognition by framing the talks as "your side, our side." This allowed the illusion of a two-sided negotiation, but with each side permitted to include additional entities as it chose. This enabled the NLF and South Vietnam to participate without having to recognize each other formally. President Thieu, however, encouraged by Republicans who feared a diplomatic breakthrough might weaken Nixon's election chances, refused to participate despite intense pressure from Johnson. The Nixon campaign established secret back channel communications with Thieu through Chinese-born American **Anna Chennault** and South Vietnamese ambassador to the United States Bui Diem, and encouraged him to delay any support for peace negotiations until after the election. This deliberate undermining of the peace process had serious consequences, as Nixon aide William Safire claimed "Nixon probably would not be president were it not for Thieu" (Safire, 1975: 88). Harriman and others urged the president to begin without Thieu's consent, but despite his frustration Johnson recognized South Vietnam's complaints. The various sides could not even agree on the shape of the negotiating table until the Johnson administration was on its way out of office. Only after Nixon won the presidency by a narrow margin did Thieu agree to join the Paris talks, though the South Vietnamese continued to drag their feet.

Even had the southerners been more cooperative, neither the United States nor North Vietnam was yet prepared to compromise on fundamental issues. Stalemate, both military and political, remained at the end of 1968. Tet persuaded many Americans that victory with acceptable costs would not be won. The United States wanted relief from the war, but no consensus existed on how best to achieve it. President Johnson had given up on military escalation while retaining the hope of meeting America's long-standing goals. A new president entered the White House pledged to find an answer.

4   The End of the Tunnel

Although Richard Nixon implied during his presidential campaign that he had a secret plan to end the war in Vietnam, his approach was less planned than spasmodic. Ultimately adopting what he called Vietnamization, Nixon presided over America's withdrawal from Vietnam, but only after an additional four years of war.

Vietnamization

Richard Nixon had long supported the war, but recognized that an increasingly divided public would not tolerate the conflict indefinitely. Concerned that the United States should maintain its credibility when making foreign policy commitments, the president wanted to end the war on his own terms, which he called "peace with honor." In Vietnam, peace with honor meant US withdrawal without the taint of defeat and preservation of an independent noncommunist South Vietnam. At the very least it would offer Thieu's government a reasonable chance of survival.

The new administration attempted to achieve this goal through its own version of fighting while negotiating. Nixon and his national security advisor, **Henry Kissinger,** entered the White House confident that a military solution was still possible and that they could end the war within a year. By removing earlier restrictions on US troops, they would apply maximum military force and rely upon Nixon's reputation as an ardent anticommunist to intimidate North Vietnam into making concessions. The president even used the threat of nuclear attack, and labeled this rhetorical excess the "madman theory."

Military changes included a bombing campaign, code-named Operation Menu, against communist camps across the Cambodian border. This action foreshadowed things to come. Fearing both a strong antiwar response and a public debate that might challenge his decision, Nixon deliberately kept this expansion of the war secret. Its unintended consequences included destabilizing Cambodian society and, ultimately, contributing to his downfall as president.

Complementing these efforts, Nixon and Kissinger initiated a diplomatic offensive. The Paris peace talks, underway since 13 May 1968,

had produced no compromise by early 1969. In fact, substantial negotiations that included all four major parties began only on 25 January
1969 when South Vietnam and the NLF joined the United States and
North Vietnam. Hanoi still demanded a total cessation of bombing prior
to serious discussions and wanted Thieu's government replaced with one
that would include the NLF. Hanoi also wanted the withdrawal of US
troops. The United States insisted on retaining the existing Saigon government and the mutual withdrawal of American and North Vietnamese troops from the South. President Thieu opposed any coalition that
would include the NLF.

To break this stalemate Nixon applied pressure on the Soviet Union as
well as his "madman" approach to the North Vietnamese. The president
hoped to use the Soviet desire for improved relations with the United
States to stimulate pressure on Hanoi to sign an agreement favorable to
the Americans. Although the losses incurred during the 1968 offensives
caused Hanoi to shift to a more cautious military strategy, North Vietnam's determination to unify the country remained undiminished.

The administration needed time for these military and diplomatic
initiatives to produce results. To build a base of popular support for
these efforts, Nixon adopted a policy borrowed from his predecessor.
This policy, which he called Vietnamization, meant turning over primary responsibility for conducting the war to the South Vietnamese. The
United States would gradually withdraw its forces while reinforcing the
Saigon government. Nixon expected that within a few years, and with
continued US assistance, it could successfully resist a North Vietnamese takeover. The president hoped that this modest de-escalation would
undermine antiwar protests and win additional latitude from the general public. It did not, however, win the endorsement of his military
commander. General Abrams strongly opposed Vietnamization as the
equivalent to surrender.

Meeting at Midway Island on 8 June 1969, Nixon informed President Thieu of the Vietnamization policy. Thieu argued for time and
resources to strengthen his armed forces. Although he believed that
Nixon would maintain a strong commitment to South Vietnam, the US
withdrawal would produce much anxiety about his country's future
over the next four years. Many Vietnamese saw the new policy as an
American evacuation. Phased withdrawals began that same month,
with the first 25,000 troops returning to the United States. Although
Nixon hoped to be completely out of Vietnam by the end of 1970, he
also indicated that US forces would stay until completion of a negotiated settlement.

Secretly, Nixon informed Ho Chi Minh in July that unless significant
progress in negotiations came by 1 November he would take "measures
of great consequence and force" (Nixon, 1978: 394). Kissinger headed a
small secret group to devise plans for a brutal assault against the North
should progress not occur. Still presuming the possibility of a military

victory, Kissinger remarked at the first meeting, "I can't believe that a fourth-rate power like North Vietnam doesn't have a breaking point" (Morris, 1977: 164). The threat had no apparent impact. Hanoi agreed to a US suggestion for private talks outside the formal discussions in Paris, but did not alter its basic demands. Cabinet members warned Nixon that military escalation would antagonize domestic opposition, and Kissinger's group concluded that their planned actions could not guarantee the desired results. With this cautionary advice and massive antiwar demonstrations in October, Nixon reluctantly backed away from his threat.

American antiwar activists were unimpressed with Nixon's efforts and, after a brief respite, escalated their protests. The idea of the Moratorium, a suspension of normal activities, originated from a Massachusetts peace group. A handful of younger activists, who included **Sam Brown** and David Hawk, began organizing in late spring 1969. The Moratorium appealed to moderates by building local actions around a one-day protest, with actions expanding one additional day each month until the war ended. The first Moratorium on 15 October exceeded the most optimistic expectations. At least one million participants made it the largest, most diverse and pervasive protest of the entire war. Citizens conducted vigils, distributed literature, attended religious services or discussion groups, showed films, held public readings of the names of war dead, or joined candlelight marches. Many of the rallies featured the repeated lines of a John Lennon song: "all we are saying is give peace a chance."

Believing that antiwar efforts undermined his pressure against North Vietnam, particularly his 1 November deadline, Nixon struck back. During a televised speech on 3 November Nixon defended the US commitment, explained his Vietnamization policy, and blatantly attacked antiwar forces. He appealed for support from the "silent majority," and concluded, "North Vietnam cannot defeat or humiliate the United States. Only Americans can do that" [**Doc. 21**]. Many observers viewed Nixon's speech as a successful political ploy. The appeal gave the president some breathing room to pursue his policy and undercut some of the movement's message. Vice-President **Spiro Agnew** followed up with increasingly bitter and divisive attacks on antiwar forces and the news media. The administration's offensive apparently succeeded, as press coverage of antiwar actions became more negative. Behind the scenes, the administration expanded government surveillance of the movement through both legal and illegal means. The FBI, CIA, and Internal Revenue Service harassed and disrupted their organizations and activities, and undercover agents sometimes instigated illegal and violent actions. Incremental troop withdrawals, reduced draft calls, and a new draft lottery system were all attempts to buy Nixon additional time through weakening dissent.

The administration's rhetorical assaults failed to deflect another massive protest just days later. In fact it drove the different ideological wings of the movement into closer cooperation. The moderate Moratorium organizers coordinated their November actions with the more radical leadership of the New Mobilization Committee. Meeting in Washington on 13–15 November, the Moratorium sponsored a religious "mass for peace" and a 36-hour March Against Death, one of the era's most moving actions. The Mobilization's rally on 15 November attracted perhaps 500,000 people.

The fall 1969 antiwar demonstrations proved to be the high point of organized dissent. Activists continued to protest, but the largest events thereafter resulted from spontaneous reactions to specific events rather than long-term planning. Both the Moratorium and the New Mobilization Committee faded by the following spring. Vietnamization brought US troop levels down to 475,000 after a year and to 335,000 by summer 1971. The withdrawals and declining US casualties helped defuse domestic protest, silence congressional critics, and strengthen Nixon's support, but they also limited American military and political options.

Vietnamization's effectiveness in Southeast Asia was harder to analyze. Efforts to strengthen South Vietnam produced some positive results. While American troops conducted ongoing operations against communist forces, US advisors increased their training of Saigon's troops. South Vietnam increased the size of its armed forces from 820,000 in 1968 to one million in 1970. At the same time, ARVN's high desertion rate of 140,000 in 1968 declined thereafter, though it remained a serious problem. The United States provided more sophisticated weapons and enormous amounts of supplies, giving the South an equipment advantage over the North. Nixon also augmented the Accelerated Pacification Campaign, assigning additional troops to village security, promoting social and political reforms, and expanding government services. By early 1970 ARVN appeared significantly improved, as did many local militia units. The combination of Hanoi's post-Tet move to a defensive strategy plus continued US military pressure made some rural areas of the South more secure than ever before. NLF recruiting and taxation became more difficult and insurgent activity had decreased. Some American observers were optimistic.

Despite occasional hopeful assessments, however, Vietnamization did not significantly alter the situation in Vietnam. Combat after 1969 generally took place in remote areas controlled by the NLF, and ARVN casualties remained high even as US deaths declined. American advice and equipment remained incapable of correcting the problems of corruption and politicization in the South Vietnamese military. US military officials generally agreed that the South Vietnamese could not withstand PAVN and PLAF regular units without American help. A Defense Department study concluded that "Without major reforms . . . it is unlikely that the

[ARVN] . . . will ever constitute an effective political or military counter to the Viet Cong" (Schlight, 1986: 148).

Traditional problems of desertion and inflated enlistment rosters that fed corrupt officers' pay compromised ARVN's apparently impressive size. Troops often distrusted Saigon, lacked adequate pay, food, and medical care, and frequently deserted because of competing responsibilities to their families. Competent officers remained in short supply, American advisors continued to note ARVN's distaste for combat, and officials at all levels wondered how the South Vietnamese could succeed where the United States had failed. The improved security in the countryside was also deceptive. Some US officials argued that it came primarily from American rather than South Vietnamese operations combined with the communists' change of strategy. Furthermore, Thieu did not prepare for conducting the war without an American military presence. His government never generated much popular enthusiasm and remained tied to a narrowly based and corrupt coalition.

By spring 1970 the weaknesses of Vietnamization began to catch up with Nixon. Continued troop withdrawals to quiet domestic opposition made progress in Vietnam more difficult. General Abrams continued to oppose the withdrawals, and negotiations had not produced any concessions from the North. Nixon looked for a new show of force to produce results.

Cambodia

Under its anti-communist head of state, Prince **Norodom Sihanouk**, Cambodia had remained neutral in the Cold War since the 1954 Geneva Conference. After dealing with both capitalist and communist powers during the 1950s to retain its independence, Cambodian policy became more anti-American with US escalation in Vietnam, and it severed diplomatic ties altogether in 1965. Communist insurgents known as the Khmer Rouge initiated an armed resistance against Sihanouk the following year. Led by **Pol Pot**, the Khmer Rouge held suspicions about Vietnamese intentions. In the meantime, the North Vietnamese had extended the Ho Chi Minh Trail through parts of eastern Cambodia and, with Sihanouk's knowledge, moved supplies from the Cambodian port of Sihanoukville. Sihanouk tolerated this violation of Cambodian territory in return for North Vietnam's neutrality toward the Khmer Rouge. President Johnson refrained from attacking North Vietnamese locations across the border, reasoning that an American invasion would lead to North Vietnam's support for the Khmer Rouge and jeopardize Sihanouk's control. Ultimately, however, the growth of the Khmer Rouge and North Vietnamese activity threatened Sihanouk's position to the point where he renewed relations with the United States. "We are a country caught between the hammer and the anvil," he told one

American writer (Karnow, 1983: 590). He privately agreed to American pursuit of Vietnamese forces into Cambodia.

In March 1969 President Nixon ordered Operation Menu, the secret bombing of Vietnamese sanctuaries inside Cambodia, hoping to slow North Vietnamese infiltration and military operations in the South. He deliberately concealed this extension of the war from Congress and the American public. Cambodia reopened diplomatic relations with the United States and, predictably, the North Vietnamese threw their support to the Khmer Rouge and strengthened their Cambodian bases.

During the spring of 1970 the Vietnam War expanded dramatically into neighboring Cambodia. On 18 March 1970 Cambodia's National Assembly ousted Sihanouk while he was out of the country, and replaced him with a pro-American faction headed by **Lon Nol**. The new government demanded the withdrawal of all Vietnamese troops from their country, restricting the flow of North Vietnamese supplies through Siha-noukville while police and military forces violently assaulted Vietnamese civilians inside the eastern Cambodian border. Following the coup, and with US instruction, South Vietnamese troops conducted cross-border operations against the NLF and PAVN, and the United States funneled secret military support to Lon Nol's government.

No longer concerned with violating a neutral country's border, Nixon supported his military's long-standing desire to attack communist bases inside Cambodia. A North Vietnamese build-up along the border posed a potential invasion threat. The president hoped that a military strike proposed by Abrams could win additional time for Vietnamization, bolster a pro-American government in Cambodia, and perhaps force concessions from the North Vietnamese at the negotiating table. He approved two combined US–South Vietnamese operations across the Cambodian border. The controversial decision stimulated objections from both Defense Secretary **Melvin Laird** and Secretary of State **William Rogers**. Nixon's announcement of the invasion to a national television audience on 30 April called it a response to North Vietnamese aggression and necessary to protect Americans in Vietnam. The key target was the Central Office for South Vietnam (COSVN), the enemy's military operations center. His exaggerated claims and rhetoric painted a vision of Armageddon [Doc. 22].

The results proved to be less than apocalyptic: 30,000 US and 50,000 South Vietnamese troops, with air and artillery support, moved into Cambodia on 30 April. The offensive leveled hundreds of acres of jungle and captured sizeable quantities of weapons and supplies. It also rendered enemy base camps temporarily unusable and increased PAVN supply problems. Vietnamization may have received a bit more time. The damage, however, was not permanent and COSVN turned out to be nothing more than "a scattering of empty huts" (Karnow, 1983: 610). The North Vietnamese returned to their bases as soon as the

Americans and the ARVN withdrew. Neither did the invasion produce any concessions at the negotiating table. The invading forces claimed 2,000 enemy deaths, but ARVN's performance underscored its reliance on American support.

The war's expansion into a neighboring country actually increased the American burden at a time when the United States was trying to reduce its involvement in Indochina. The attack pushed the North Vietnamese deeper into Cambodia and drove them into closer cooperation with the Khmer Rouge. Additional US resources now flowed to yet another weak and unstable ally dependent upon the United States for its survival. This American invasion bears at least partial responsibility for the escalation of Cambodia's civil war that resulted in a Khmer Rouge victory. For Cambodia, the end of neutrality would have catastrophic results.

Domestically, the Cambodian invasion produced some of the war's most extensive and tragic protests. Nixon recognized that this controversial decision would infuriate domestic doves, but he underestimated the emotion that it unleashed. The antiwar movement reacted quickly to this expansion of the war, particularly on college campuses. At Kent State University in Ohio, on 4 May 1970, National Guardsmen fired into a crowd, killing four people and wounding nine others. Over 500 college campuses closed down in the following days, and nearly 100,000 protesters converged on Washington on 9 May. The next week Mississippi police killed two more students at Jackson State University. Although polls showed that many Americans supported the Cambodian invasion, the massive public demonstrations limited Nixon's options. The public would not tolerate any expansion of a war they believed was winding down.

An independent Chicano antiwar movement identified with the Vietnamese war against colonialism, questioned the drafting of Mexican Americans, and examined the war's domestic impact on Chicanos, employing the slogan *La batalla esta aqui* ("The battle is here"). The largest Chicano Moratorium March took place in Los Angeles on 29 August 1970, drawing as many as 30,000 participants. The event ended tragically when police incited a confrontation that resulted in three deaths and 152 arrests (Oropeza, 2005: 170).

Congress, which was largely kept in the dark about the Cambodian operation, reacted with a rare rebuke. In June the Senate overwhelmingly voted to repeal the Gulf of Tonkin Resolution. The Cooper–Church amendment proposed cutting off US funds for American troops in Cambodia after 30 June, and the Hatfield–McGovern amendment called for withdrawing US forces from Vietnam by the end of 1971. Nixon hit back at his opponents, blaming them for prolonging the war. He also briefly endorsed the Huston Plan, which proposed widespread violations of civil liberties to attack his political opponents. The president managed to survive this crisis. He pulled US troops out of Cambodia by late June, defusing most of the congressional and antiwar pressure. The House of Representatives rejected the Cooper–Church amendment, while both the Senate and House voted down Hatfield–McGovern.

Even while antagonizing his political opposition, however, Nixon felt limited by its strength. The Cambodian invasion did not produce the desired result and the deadlock remained. North Vietnam refused to attend the Paris negotiations until US troops were out of Cambodia and suspended the secret talks even longer. Hanoi remained patient, and time for the United States was running out. Congress prohibited US ground troops from further actions in Cambodia or Laos.

After two years in office, Nixon's policies had produced nothing new in Vietnam, and domestic pressure to end the war continued from both the antiwar movement and Congress. Saigon's position seemed stable, but enemy infiltration increased at the end of 1970. Even though Vietnamization remained suspect, Nixon continued the troop withdrawals to ease domestic pressures. By the end of 1971 only 175,000 American troops remained in Vietnam. To offset this reduction in ground troops, he escalated the air war against North Vietnam, Laos, and Cambodia.

Laos

The war spilled over again in 1971. Since 1962 the United States had supported the neutral Laotian government of **Souvanna Phouma**. The CIA trained and equipped mountain tribes, especially the Hmong, to fight against communist insurgents. North Vietnam backed the Laotian communists, known as the Pathet Lao, and the Ho Chi Minh Trail ran through eastern Laos. Between 1964 and 1968, the United States had dropped nearly a half-billion tons of bombs in Laos as Lyndon Johnson quietly initiated bombing to interdict North Vietnamese supply routes. Under Nixon the bombing of Laos increased.

On 30 January 1971 US air and artillery forces supported a South Vietnamese invasion of Laos. Known as Operation Lam Son 719, the invasion came after US intelligence concluded that the stockpiling of material in Laos indicated a possible communist attack against South Vietnam's northern provinces sometime in 1972. Lam Son 719 would disrupt North Vietnamese supply lines and base camps to prevent the invasion before US troop levels were too low to provide the necessary support.

ARVN's invasion was disappointing at best. On 8 February the first of 21,000 South Vietnamese troops moved into Laos and gradually advanced to take their target, the town of Tchepone, on 6 March. They found it flattened by American bombs. Withdrawing after six weeks in Laos, ARVN faced 36,000 PAVN troops and Russian-made tanks in some of the bloodiest fighting of the war. The withdrawal quickly turned into a rout, and the South Vietnamese left tanks, artillery, and other equipment behind in their flight.

US officials claimed 15,000 enemy killed and enough supplies destroyed to postpone the planned enemy offensive, creating additional time for Vietnamization to work. ARVN, however, suffered 50 percent casualties, including 2,000 dead, and performed below expectations. Without American air power things would have been much worse. The chaotic retreat again raised serious questions about the success of Vietnamization. The PAVN had bloodied some of the best units in a well-equipped army. General Abrams' assessment was that ARVN was unable to "sustain large scale major cross border operations . . . without external support" (Clarke, 1988: 473). The Laotian invasion reassured the North that it could deal with ARVN even with US air support. Hanoi absorbed the Laotian setback and built toward a 1972 offensive.

Much like the previous spring, a series of events challenged the war following the Laotian invasion. On 29 March 1971 a court-martial convicted Lieutenant **William Calley** of multiple murders. Calley's actions took place during a 1968 massacre by American troops of nearly 500 unarmed Vietnamese civilians at My Lai. Although the Army tried to cover up the incident, the *New York Times* finally broke the story in November 1969. The trial split the nation between those who defended the killings as an act of war, those who criticized the massacre as murder, and others who saw Calley as a scapegoat who suffered while higher-ranking officials avoided responsibility. Originally sentenced to life in prison, Calley received a reduced sentence on appeal and eventually received parole after serving three years.

Calley's conviction came two months after a public investigation of American war crimes conducted by the Vietnam Veterans Against the War (VVAW). Testimony from their Winter Soldier Investigation, held in Detroit from 31 January through 2 February 1971, indicated that My Lai was not a unique event. Although most Americans discounted accusations of war crimes, the VVAW's presence in Washington DC during several days of spring demonstrations brought increased notoriety and legitimacy to the movement [**Doc. 23**]. In April 1971, hundreds of military veterans threw away their medals on the steps of the US Capitol building. An early May attempt by several thousand radicals to block city streets and shut down the capital failed. The courts ruled, however, that the massive government sweep that arrested over 12,000 protesters was illegal.

The antiwar movement proved extremely unpopular even as public opinion increasingly adopted an antiwar stance. The reasons for this are complex, but distorted media coverage accounts for a significant part of it (Hall, 2012: 132). Despite government and right-wing efforts to associate the movement with communism and the radical left, the CIA concluded that "diversity is the most striking single characteristic of the peace movement . . ." (DeBenedetti, 1983: 35). Demonstrators developed a wide range of actions and events to make their arguments.

Weakened by factionalism and countercultural modes of protest, activists nevertheless generally interpreted their dissent as part of America's most admirable past. Their consistent presence forced government decision makers to consider public dissent as they plotted strategy, even while discounting its impact publicly. The movement restricted military escalation at certain key points while proving unable to stop the war unilaterally.

The government's credibility on the war suffered with the exposure of a secret government study on wartime decision-making. On 13 June 1971 the *New York Times* began publishing excerpts of what became known as *The Pentagon Papers*. Leaked to the press by **Daniel Ellsberg**, a Defense Department analyst, these documents showed that American leaders ignored international agreements, manipulated Saigon governments, and lied to Congress and the public. The public finally had evidence to support critics' assertions of government deception regarding Vietnam. President Nixon tried to stop their publication, but the Supreme Court ruled against him. *The Pentagon Papers* created greater public disillusionment and decreased tolerance for an extended commitment.

Negotiations

Having accepted the improbability of a military victory, Nixon's negotiations with the Vietnamese focused on establishing conditions for American withdrawal. The South Vietnamese would have to work out any military solution themselves. A secret proposal through Kissinger in May 1971 offered an American withdrawal within seven months of a cease-fire and the return of American POWs. Nixon also dropped his insistence that North Vietnamese troops withdraw from the South, demanding only that they end further infiltration. Hanoi rejected the offer, unwilling to accept the Thieu regime or end the fighting, which served as its main bargaining chip. North Vietnam's chief negotiator, Le Duc Tho, countered by offering to release POWs concurrently with an American withdrawal if the United States dropped its support for Thieu. Kissinger declined.

Peace talks stalled over the maintenance of Thieu's government. The North had long insisted on his removal before accepting a final political settlement. Each side felt it had invested too much time and blood to concede any fundamental demands as long as there remained a chance to win their goals on the battlefield. The North was planning a major 1972 offensive, while Nixon had scheduled summit meetings with both China and the Soviet Union. Not until these final efforts failed would a negotiated peace finally be possible.

By the early 1970s the United States pursued a negotiated settlement in part because of the deterioration of its armed forces. The American military in Vietnam faced declining morale and growing discipline problems after the imposition of Vietnamization blurred the war's continued purpose. As US withdrawals increased, drug abuse, racial tension, and attacks against unpopular officers known as "fragging" all escalated to the point where some questioned the Army's effectiveness. After 1968, illegal drug use developed into a near epidemic. A Department of Defense study indicated that 60 percent of US military personnel in Vietnam used drugs in 1970, a figure that grew to 70 percent by 1973. The most common drugs were marijuana and amphetamines, but opium and heroin were also widely used. The US Army desertion rate hit an all-time high in 1971. From 1963 to 1973 a half-million soldiers deserted, nearly 20 percent of those were gone for more than a month. By comparison, the South Vietnamese Army counted 570,000 deserters from 1967 to 1971, and during the same time period the PAVN/NLF lost 87,000. Facing this reality, General Abrams confided to an aide, "I need to get this army home to save it" (Sorley, 1999: 289).

Pacification

Despite greater attention to pacification efforts after 1968, the Americans and South Vietnamese achieved only minimal results. They made greater efforts to control territory, used rural development teams for village administration and construction, offered amnesty programs to the enemy, land reform for the peasants, and returned more political power to village councils.

The Phoenix Program attempted to eliminate the NLF's political structure by identifying and arresting its political cadres. Phoenix grew out of a 1967 CIA pacification effort that began coordinating with the South Vietnamese in 1968. In many areas this program effectively weakened the NLF. From 1968 to 1972, when Phoenix was phased out, operatives captured 34,000 and killed 26,000 people. The high number of deaths brought criticism from several quarters that the Phoenix Program functioned as an assassination project. While effective, Phoenix did not destroy the NLF, and its tactics often stimulated new support for the insurgents. Like many pacification efforts, Phoenix suffered from corruption and inefficiency. Officials arrested innocent people to meet quotas and allowed many of those captured to bribe their way to freedom. Later studies indicate that most of the gains associated with the Phoenix Program emerged from American military actions and Hanoi's temporary reversion to protracted war rather than significant improvements in South Vietnamese security forces. The withdrawal of American troops during Vietnamization hurt the program, and a 1971 Pentagon study called it "only marginally effective." A CIA operative identified it less kindly as "thought of by geniuses and implemented by idiots" (Isaacs, 1983: 108).

The main problem with these pacification efforts was that they came too late, attempted a quick solution, and ignored fundamental problems within the government. The communists' long history of working in rural areas, plus Saigon's isolation from the countryside, made new efforts more difficult. Real progress demanded time, and there was no time. The corruption and political intrigue that damaged military effectiveness also damaged pacification.

The Easter Offensive

Since the 1968 Tet Offensive, North Vietnam had anticipated conducting another major campaign. In late 1971 Le Duan pressed General Giap to call for a general offensive and uprising for early 1972. Northern leaders assumed that South Vietnam was vulnerable because of its poor showing in Laos the previous spring. Rather than attack the major cities as before, Hanoi targeted ARVN forces, hoping to undermine Vietnamization and permit NLF cadres to regain the initiative in the countryside before the final peace negotiations. The North Vietnamese further assumed that Nixon, pressed by domestic political concerns to end the war before the November presidential election, would be unable to send additional forces to reinforce the 95,000 US troops that still remained.

One additional factor in Hanoi's decision to push for a quicker end to the war was the changing relations between the United States and the major communist powers. Nixon shockingly negotiated personal visits to both China and the Soviet Union in February and May of 1972. He hoped this pursuit of global *détente* would allow the United States to extricate itself from Vietnam. North Vietnamese leaders were concerned about being ignored in this great-power diplomacy. Northerners remembered the restrained support they received from the Soviet Union and China during the 1954 Geneva Conference. They were understandably anxious about strained relations between Vietnam's major benefactors and the resulting contest for influence in Southeast Asia. The extra factor of improved relations with the United States could make both the Chinese and Soviets susceptible to American pressures to coerce North Vietnam into accepting a negotiated settlement on American terms. Hoping to avoid a repeat of the Geneva disappointment, Hanoi wanted to weaken Nixon's diplomatic efforts and prevent potential isolation and loss of aid from its two primary benefactors. At a minimum, the North believed a major offensive would improve its negotiating position and undercut Vietnamization by inflicting heavy losses and eroding southern morale. At best, they hoped to defeat ARVN, overthrow Thieu's government, and force the Americans to withdraw.

The North Vietnamese launched the Easter Offensive, a major conventional invasion of the South, on 30 March 1972. The three-pronged

assault included nearly 120,000 PAVN regulars, joined by PLAF guerrillas and led by Soviet-built tanks. They poured across the DMZ into the
northern provinces, targeted the central highlands, and moved over the
Cambodian border into the region northwest of Saigon. The Americans
were once again caught completely unprepared, and had seriously underestimated the enemy's capabilities. Only days before the attack, Secretary
of Defense Melvin Laird claimed that a major invasion was "not a serious
possibility" (Karnow, 1983: 640). Communist troops swept aside ARVN
forces as they captured Quang Tri in the north and moved against Hue.
Forces in the highlands threatened Kontum while the southern attack
targeted An Loc. When Thieu sent most of his reserves to defend those
cities, the PLAF launched an offensive in the Mekong delta and around
Saigon.

The United States responded quickly, and again American air power
was decisive. Nixon eliminated restrictions in place since late 1968 and
renewed air attacks on North Vietnam. B-52s struck across the DMZ
and in the Hanoi–Haiphong area. Known as Operation Linebacker, the
continuous attacks hit nearly every target with military value. Henry
Kissinger pressed the Soviets to rein in the Vietnamese, and informed
them of US willingness to permit northern troops to remain in the South
after a cease-fire. When North Vietnam rejected the offer, Nixon ignored
reservations from cabinet officials and Kissinger and struck back hard
with the biggest escalation of the war since 1965. He ordered massive
bombing, a naval blockade of the North, and the mining of Haiphong
harbor, previously denied for fear of creating an incident with Soviet
ships.

The American response threatened *détente*, but the Soviets did not cancel their upcoming summit meeting with Nixon. Both the Soviet Union
and China formally protested against US actions, but also encouraged
North Vietnam to reach a peace settlement. Hanoi's perception that
great-power diplomacy was more important than Vietnam was certainly
correct, especially for the Chinese, whose support for Hanoi had declined
after 1968. Nixon also enjoyed a relatively calm domestic response. Criticism both within and outside government was not as widespread or as
heated as in the past.

Operation Linebacker may have prevented a devastating defeat for
South Vietnam. As the heaviest bombing of the war, it seriously damaged North Vietnamese fuel and ammunition storage sites and harassed
supply lines. Aerial combat support enabled ARVN to hold off assaults
on Kontum and An Loc. In the northern provinces the South Vietnamese held Hue, then counterattacked against Quang Tri, relying on massive
firepower from artillery and US bombers. Only after a ground assault and
five days of heavy fighting did ARVN retake the city on 15 September,
ten weeks after the offensive began. Quang Tri was left, as one journalist
described, "a lake of shattered masonry" (Isaacs, 1983: 26).

Hanoi found the results of the Easter Offensive disappointing. The North sustained heavy losses; more than 100,000 deaths compared with South Vietnam's 30,000 killed and over 90,000 wounded or missing. It had underestimated ARVN's abilities and America's quick response. Nevertheless, its military capabilities remained intact. American withdrawals and Nixon's pursuit of *détente* made Saigon anxious about its long-term support. Although southern morale had declined and ARVN still appeared vulnerable, Thieu remained in power. Neither side gained a significant advantage during the spring. Once again Le Duan's general offensive strategy had failed to change the military balance and Hanoi finally gave priority to reaching a diplomatic resolution. North Vietnam was unable to drive the United States out of Indochina, but nor was the United States able to end the Vietnamese revolution.

By late 1972 both sides faced circumstances that made a diplomatic solution possible. Both were frustrated in trying to win a military advantage and neither was confident of breaking the stalemate and prevailing. Nixon and Kissinger faced continued domestic pressure, but also believed the war in Vietnam hindered their maneuvers with China and the Soviet Union. The North Vietnamese received less consistent support from the Chinese and Soviets and suffered tremendously during the Easter Offensive. Assuming that Nixon would win his presidential race, they expected more advantageous terms prior to the election.

The Paris Agreement

By mid-1972 both North Vietnam and the United States recognized that their objectives could not soon be attained on the battlefield. Finally accepting the necessity of compromise, they moved toward a negotiated settlement. Thieu's government, however, recognized that any American compromise threatened its existence and fought against a settlement. Henry Kissinger and Le Duc Tho resumed their secret talks in the summer. Having already abandoned its demand that North Vietnamese troops withdraw from the South, by late September the United States indicated some flexibility in its support of Thieu. Hanoi reciprocated by dropping its insistence that Thieu's government step down and called instead for a coalition government that would recognize and include the NLF, now designated as the People's Revolutionary Government (PRG).

On 8 October Le Duc Tho proposed a framework that Kissinger found acceptable. It called for a cease-fire, with the respective armies retaining their areas of control. Within 60 days, the United States would withdraw its troops and both sides would exchange prisoners of war. A tripartite commission, composed of the Saigon government, the PRG, and a nonaligned faction, would negotiate a political settlement after the cease-fire. Those negotiations would address democratic elections in the South, eventual unification of Vietnam by peaceful means, and a US contribution to postwar reconstruction. Though some issues remained unresolved, they reached a preliminary agreement that same month, and Kissinger prepared to discuss the agreement with Nixon and Thieu. Nixon saw political advantages to waiting until after the election and wanted to delay a final settlement.

South Vietnamese leaders were furious that the United States had reached an agreement without consulting them. They opposed leaving northern troops in southern territory and the implied establishment of a coalition government. Thieu recognized his vulnerability with the proposed agreement and refused to sign. Hanoi officials suspected that the United States was using Thieu to back out of the agreement and publicly accused the Americans of abandoning the deal. Fearful that the settlement might be slipping away, Kissinger misleadingly declared on 31 October that "peace is at hand."

Following Nixon's re-election, the United States and North Vietnam reconvened in Paris on 21 November to negotiate the South Vietnamese objections. Kissinger presented Thieu's demands for 69 changes, but Hanoi insisted on the October agreement. After three weeks of unsuccessful discussions, Nixon blamed the difficulties on Hanoi. Talks broke off on 13 December.

Hoping to bolster Saigon's fighting capabilities after America's imminent departure, Nixon initiated Operation Enhance Plus, a massive concentrated infusion of military equipment and supplies. This funneled hundreds of aircraft and armored vehicles to South Vietnam to strengthen its military and persuade Thieu to sign the agreement. Nixon further provided private assurance that the United States would intervene with military force if North Vietnam violated the agreement.

Partly to pressure North Vietnam into making concessions and returning to the negotiating table, but largely to reassure Thieu of America's commitment, Nixon launched Operation Linebacker II on 18 December. Commonly called the Christmas Bombing, this massive eleven-day aerial assault targeted the Hanoi and Haiphong regions, and was the most intensive of the entire war. Using B-52s for the first time on the North's main cities, it disrupted northern supply lines and, in conjunction with an earlier blockade, cut North Vietnamese supply imports by 80 percent. The bombing produced international outrage. Criticism of the bombing came not only from China, but also from America's Western allies and the American public. Nixon's approval rating plummeted to 39 percent. Despite the criticism of terror bombing, however, the 1,600 civilian deaths were significantly less than some other air attacks. The United States suffered its heaviest loss of aircraft of the war, losing 26 planes, including 15 B-52s, and 92 airmen. On 26 December Hanoi indicated its willingness to reopen talks on 8 January, and the bombing stopped on 30 December.

Although Nixon and Kissinger claimed that the bombing forced North Vietnam back to the bargaining table with new concessions, most analysts disagree. The United States, North Vietnam, South Vietnam, and the PRG signed the Paris Agreement on 27 January 1973. The final settlement closely resembled the October document. Thieu agreed only under Nixon's threat to sign the agreement without him. The fundamental issue of South Vietnam's political situation remained unresolved. America's military withdrawal and the continued presence of North Vietnamese troops left Thieu's position weakened, but his government still remained. The United States had finally found a way out of Vietnam, though it did not achieve Nixon's "peace with honor." The Paris Agreement only thinly disguised the reality that the United States had failed to end the threat to Saigon's existence. Hanoi was temporarily content with the arrangements, which allowed it to rest from decades of devastation and to maintain its goal of national unification. The agreement clearly favored the objective of the North Vietnamese.

5 Conclusion and Legacy

As officials signed the Paris Agreement in January 1973, few Vietnamese leaders of any political persuasion believed that it represented more than a brief cease-fire while the Americans departed. Hanoi remained determined to unify the country under its direction while Saigon intended to maintain itself as an independent state. Anticipating a renewed political and military struggle, in the last days before the agreement took effect both sides maneuvered to extend their influence over the countryside.

The American Withdrawal

Nixon had promised to maintain "full economic and military aid" and to "react strongly" if North Vietnam violated the Paris Agreement (Nixon, 1978: 749), a commitment he reaffirmed when Thieu visited the United States in April 1973. This arrangement, however, carried no legal obligation and had no public consensus behind it. The United States transferred its military bases and a massive amount of supplies and equipment to South Vietnam before the cease-fire took effect. As the United States withdrew its personnel and reduced its flow of resources, however, Saigon proved unable to stand for long on its own. The Watergate scandal and America's national war weariness left Nixon unable to fulfill his informal arrangements with President Thieu.

In addition to the Paris Agreement, Nixon had also secretly agreed to provide up to $4.75 billion over five years to aid North Vietnam's reconstruction [Doc. 26]. He used the threat of withholding this money and of renewed US military intervention to keep the communists from violating the agreement. Whether Nixon actually intended to make this payment or not, North Vietnam never received any reconstruction aid.

By 26 March 1973 North Vietnam released 591 US prisoners of war, and American combat troops had withdrawn. South Vietnam freed nearly 27,000 prisoners, though the communists claimed that 15,000 remained imprisoned. The communists returned over 5,300 South Vietnamese. Further negotiations eventually led to additional releases. Only 159 US Marines remained to guard the American embassy, although many of the nearly 10,000 American civilians who stayed behind had been hastily discharged from the military so they could remain.

Nixon lost some of his flexibility in shaping Indochinese policy as Congress asserted greater control. Reflecting a national weariness with Vietnam, it condemned the ongoing bombing of Cambodia as illegal, and the House of Representatives cut off funds for additional air missions. Congress also refused to provide aid to North Vietnam without a full accounting of Americans missing in action (MIA). An October 1973 war in the Middle East and ongoing revelations implicating Nixon in the Watergate scandal pushed events in Vietnam further into the background and weakened the president's authority. Watergate grew out of a burglary of the Democratic National Committee offices that was part of a series of illegal and unethical activities perpetrated by the Nixon administration to destroy its political enemies. Public enthusiasm for the Vietnam War had long dissipated. Though Nixon vetoed a bill immediately ending all military operations in Indochina, Congress forced a compromise deadline of 15 August. Overriding another veto, Congress passed the War Powers Act on 7 November in an effort to acquire greater influence in committing the nation's military forces.

The Paris Agreement allowed the United States to extricate its forces from Vietnam, but it did virtually nothing to settle Vietnam's political differences. Since neither Hanoi nor Saigon was willing to compromise its fundamental goals, the prisoner exchange stood as one of the agreement's few achievements. The cease-fire quickly broke down as both sides committed frequent violations. The Saigon government claimed control of 75 percent of southern territory. Its armed forces of nearly one million soldiers outnumbered the PAVN and PLAF in the South by roughly ten to one. Thieu used this advantage soon after the cease-fire to retake areas recently occupied by the PRG. Within three months the South Vietnamese managed to recover most of the hamlets taken in the weeks before the Paris Agreement.

The communists moved more cautiously. During the first part of the year they regrouped from the arduous campaigns of 1972 and strengthened their political control. Communist military units refused to engage ARVN when possible unless they held clear superiority. They took precautions to avoid any actions that might lead the United States to reintroduce its own troops or renew the bombing. All of this served as preparation for the war's renewal. Tens of thousands of additional troops infiltrated into the South via the Ho Chi Minh Trail. With improved supply lines and larger numbers, by late 1973 communist forces regained some of their traditional strongholds in the Mekong delta.

Saigon's territorial claims often exaggerated its ability to govern and defend villages, overestimated the villagers' acceptance of Saigon's authority, and ignored the PRG's control of those areas at night. Thieu continued to avoid reforms that might attract peasant loyalty. Government corruption often meant that the system ran on bribery, and that was particularly true within the military. The armed forces, which represented Thieu's strongest political base, suffered not only from corruption, but had their effectiveness eroded by heavy casualties and desertions during their 1973 offensives. The decline in US aid also made it more difficult to wage war in their American-trained style, as they encountered shortages of gasoline, ammunition, and spare parts.

South Vietnam further suffered from economic woes. A poor harvest throughout Southeast Asia created a rice shortage in 1972, and the 1974 global recession drove oil prices to new heights. At the same time the American exit had an enormous impact on South Vietnam. Correspondent Arnold Isaacs compared conditions to the American Great Depression. By 1974 the US withdrawal eliminated 300,000 jobs, costing South Vietnam $300 million per year. Concurrently, American aid fell from $2.3 billion to $1 billion. Inflation and unemployment reached staggering proportions in 1973 and 1974, creating an economic crisis that damaged morale and tragically intensified corruption. Underpaid soldiers often stole for survival, some pilots demanded bribes before flying missions to support infantry units, and the entire system generated widespread dissatisfaction with Thieu's government. Corruption, military decline, reduced US aid, and internal political dissension plagued the Saigon government. After 20 years of American nation building, South Vietnam still lacked a firm foundation.

The Final Offensives

Vietnamese efforts to reach a permanent political settlement went nowhere during 1973. President Thieu pursued a policy known as the "Four No's": no negotiations with the communists; no coalition government; no loss of territory; and no communist activity in South Vietnam. Hoping to take advantage of the South's numerical and technological superiority, and believing that American aid would continue to flow, ARVN conducted offensive operations during the remainder of 1973. The fighting peaked in October as both sides contested territory along the coast and in the Mekong delta. The heaviest fighting took place in the regions around Saigon. South Vietnamese forces slightly improved their position during much of the year.

North Vietnam faced some difficulties before fully renewing its war effort. Le Duan and Pham Van Dong were initially cautious over the possible return of US forces, but full-scale war returned by the end of 1973 and the balance tipped toward Hanoi in 1974. Le Duan traveled to the Soviet Union and China in June 1973, seeking additional aid, but found the communist powers more interested in developing better relations with the United States than in North Vietnamese victory. Hanoi's political leaders rejected launching a major offensive against the South in the fall of 1973, preferring to utilize "revolutionary violence" against Saigon's military operations. This guerrilla warfare was designed to ensure that the Americans stayed away.

South Vietnamese leaders, recognizing their continued reliance upon American support, grew increasingly anxious about the US commitment after Nixon's 9 August 1974 resignation. President **Gerald Ford** tried to reassure them that he would follow Nixon's policies, but he had no clear consensus behind him. Certainly the American public was not enthusiastic about maintaining a significant commitment and preferred to let the Vietnamese settle the conflict themselves. Congress grew more reluctant to spend additional money on Vietnam, and viewed Ambassador **Graham Martin**'s optimistic reports with skepticism. In September, Congress approved only $700 million in aid to Saigon. The reduced aid further diminished ARVN's effectiveness, which contributed to declining morale and soaring desertion rates in 1974. By the end of the year Saigon's forces were stretched thin over nearly all of South Vietnam.

In October 1974 deteriorating economic conditions and government corruption produced Catholic, Buddhist, and leftist demonstrations in Saigon and other cities. Although Thieu made some concessions by firing corrupt military leaders and cabinet officials, a hard line against public protests quieted the dissenters by November.

The South's problems coincided with a shift in northern strategy. In late 1974 leaders in Hanoi prepared for offensive operations against South Vietnam that were designed to end the war in two years. They anticipated once again that they might stimulate a general uprising against the Thieu government. North Vietnam remained uncertain about America's reaction to such an effort, assuming that the United States would not reintroduce ground troops but anticipating possible bombing attacks. In mid-December communist troops launched a major assault on Phuoc Long province in the central highlands, avoiding the more heavily defended northern provinces. On 6 January they captured the capital and soon controlled the entire province, killing or capturing nearly 5,000 ARVN troops. The American failure to respond at Phuoc Long inspired confidence among northerners that the United States would not return.

North Vietnamese troops proceeded to their main objective, Ban Me Thuot in the central highlands. They attacked on 10 March and captured the city four days later. Other forces advanced toward Pleiku and Kontum. South Vietnamese losses in the central provinces led Thieu on 13 March to order a military withdrawal to a defensive line just north of Saigon, abandoning the northern portion of his country. The unexpected change in strategy left the ARVN both angry and demoralized, and initiated a panic among both soldiers and civilians. The withdrawal quickly turned into a rout. Pleiku and Kontum fell within a week and the South Vietnamese Army began to disintegrate as thousands of soldiers deserted to try to save their families and themselves. Nearly a half-million refugees poured toward coastal cities such as Da Nang, hoping for evacuation to the South.

With the unexpectedly easy victories in the highlands and South Vietnam's apparent collapse, Hanoi officials sensed that they might be able to topple Thieu's government before the rainy season arrived and made military operations extremely difficult. The North Vietnamese revised their goals and pushed toward Saigon in the newly named Ho Chi Minh Campaign. Hue fell to the communists on 26 March and Da Nang four days later as civilian refugees and military deserters acted out a repeat of the collapse in the highlands.

Americans were shocked at the speed of South Vietnam's collapse, but resigned themselves to the outcome and no longer believed that Vietnam involved vital national interests. Congress rejected President Ford's request for $300 million in military aid the day Ban Me Thuot fell. Having suffered years of warfare and caught in the middle of an economic recession, the Americans were not inclined to spend more on Vietnam. Ford chose not to intervene with American naval or air forces. During the first week of April 1975, Army Chief of Staff **Frederick Weyand** returned from a trip to Vietnam to assess the military situation at Ford's request. Even if American aid was increased, he concluded, the Saigon government's hope to survive was "marginal at best," though he thought US troops might be needed to evacuate the last Americans and Vietnamese associates from Saigon (Schulzinger, 1997: 322–3). The CIA delivered a similarly pessimistic report. President Ford made an additional request for $722 million in military aid on 10 April. Congress remained unconvinced that the money would prevent a communist victory, but finally authorized $300 million in humanitarian aid and for the evacuation of Americans.

North Vietnamese troops moved from Da Nang to Saigon in less than a month, meeting strong resistance only at Xuan Loc in mid-April. With North Vietnamese victory all but assured, President Thieu resigned on 21 April and fled the country, bitterly denouncing the United States for South Vietnam's demise [Doc. 27]. Tran Van Huong replaced Thieu briefly before giving way a week later to General Duong Van Minh. Hanoi refused Minh's offer of a cease-fire.

Some American officials, especially Ambassador Martin, had mistakenly believed that South Vietnam could defend itself to the end and bring about a negotiated settlement. Martin delayed the American evacuation until the communists were at the gates of Saigon. United States helicopters hastily lifted over 7,000 people, 900 of them Americans, to awaiting aircraft carriers. The desperate removal of personnel from the US embassy roof provided many Americans with a final bitter memory of the nation's long involvement in Indochina. Saigon fell on 30 April 1975.

It had taken North Vietnam only 55 days for its two-year offensive to succeed [Doc. 28].

The United States shares considerable blame for the manner in which the war ended. The Americans never succeeded in building a viable nation in the South. Having taken on the burden of defending Saigon when it appeared too weak to defend itself, the United States tired of the war and turned it back over to South Vietnam. The Paris Agreement, Nixon's private arrangements with Thieu, and Congress's reduced financial support all weakened South Vietnam's chances for survival. Ultimately, however, the results were primarily determined in Vietnam. President Thieu's unwillingness to negotiate with Hanoi and his military and political blunders would have probably resulted in the same outcome regardless of American actions. South Vietnam ultimately fell because its governments never effectively escaped their colonial associations; it suffered from deep social, cultural, and political divisions; and it lacked competent leadership. Saigon was never able to stand by itself, so dependent upon the United States that when America's commitment waned there was little to prevent its collapse. Despite its own errors, massive losses, and internal divisions, North Vietnam prevailed because of superior leadership that was diplomatically skilled, its remarkably resilient people, and its identification with Vietnamese nationalism and social reform. Better organized and more strongly motivated, the North Vietnamese used the strategy of protracted war to prevail against the Americans.

The war claimed an enormous price. The communists admit to 1.1 million deaths from 1954 to 1975. They also estimate the loss of two million additional civilian casualties, although the United States calculates 30,000 deaths from the bombing of the North. A conservative estimate of South Vietnamese military deaths is over 110,000, plus nearly a half-million wounded and 415,000 civilian deaths. The United States sustained over 58,000 dead and 153,000 wounded. Other nations allied with the United States suffered over 5,200 deaths, the large majority of them South Korean.

Laos and Cambodia

The conclusion of the war in Vietnam meant that communist-led insurgencies had prevailed throughout Indochina. The Laotian civil war ended with the communist Pathet Lao in control. Despite having an officially neutral coalition government since 1962, both the North Vietnamese and the Americans had continued their support to Laotian rivals. The United States dropped over two million tons of bombs on Laos and the CIA supported a guerrilla army from the Hmong tribe. North Vietnam collaborated with the Pathet Lao and used Laotian territory. The United States, however, had always linked its support of the royal government to its presence in Vietnam. In the face of shrinking American support, the royal government negotiated a new coalition in February 1973 that gave the Pathet Lao equal status. With the collapse of South Vietnam, the Pathet Lao, aided by North Vietnam, seized control of the entire country by August 1975. The communists wiped out an estimated 100,000 Hmong and sent 20,000 supporters of the old regime to "re-education camps."

Laotian friendship proved to be the exception for Vietnam in the immediate postwar period. Elsewhere in Southeast Asia the Vietnamese struggled for power against historical rivals, regardless of communist ideology. In Cambodia the United States contributed $400 million in aid and, until Congress stopped it in August 1973, an extensive bombing campaign to the Lon Nol government. Ultimately, Lon Nol's forces collapsed, and the Americans evacuated the capital of Phnom Penh less than a week before it fell to the Khmer Rouge on 17 April 1975. The war had killed 700,000 people and created refugees of nearly 50 percent of the population. The Khmer Rouge drove everyone out of Cambodia's largest cities into the countryside to obliterate the existing society. Their revolution plunged Cambodia into a cataclysm. Headed by Pol Pot, the Khmer Rouge's genocidal programs and slave labor camps produced malnutrition, disease, and executions that killed at least one million people during its five-year rule.

Khmer Rouge attacks across the Vietnamese border over disputed territorial claims, plus the crush of 375,000 Cambodian refugees fleeing to Vietnam, produced added strains on Vietnam's already struggling economy. China's termination of aid to Vietnam in 1978, and its strong ties to Cambodia, led Hanoi to seek military support from the Soviet Union. In return for their help, the Soviets received control over the naval base at Cam Ranh Bay. To resolve the ongoing tensions with the Khmer Rouge, the Vietnamese invaded Cambodia on 25 December 1978 to a generally appreciative population. They captured Phnom Penh on 7 January 1979 and placed **Heng Samrin**, a pro-Vietnamese Cambodian communist, in control. An occupation force of 140,000 troops remained as the conflict continued.

In retaliation for attacking its client state, China invaded northern Vietnam in early 1979, but withdrew after a month. Despite Vietnam's role in ending the Cambodian genocide, Japan and several Western nations opposed the invasion and withheld economic aid from Vietnam. Neither the United States nor Southeast Asia's noncommunist countries recognized the new Cambodian government. By backing the anti-Vietnamese Cambodians in their guerrilla war against the new government, the United States ironically found itself allied with China and the Khmer Rouge. Vietnam was effectively isolated economically and grew more dependent upon the Soviet Union. By the late 1980s, having lost 50,000 casualties in Cambodia and having suffered economic deprivation, Hanoi looked for a compromise solution that would end the embargo.

Vietnamese troops finally left only after a 1991 United Nations agreement for a new Cambodian coalition government.

Impact on the United States

After 1975 the US government maintained a hostile position toward Vietnam and, especially after 1978, tried to isolate it from other nations. American citizens viewed Vietnam with a mixture of apathy and bitterness. Many Americans seemed content to forget the experience, and for a time Vietnam faded from public debate. America's 2.7 million Vietnam veterans generally returned home without fanfare, facing indifference or hostility as often as praise. Many resented their treatment and some found readjustment to civilian life difficult. Defeat left the country feeling frustrated and angry, and few were concerned with normalizing relations. President Ford reflected a common view and continued to treat Vietnam as an enemy. He imposed a trade embargo against all of Vietnam and Cambodia, and opposed Vietnam's entry into the United Nations. For years American influence kept Vietnam from developing significant economic ties with the West, leaving it to suffer even greater dependence upon the Soviet Union.

Among the most hotly contested issues of the postwar period was whether to grant amnesty to draft resisters and deserters. Former antiwar activists pointed out the country's tradition of postwar reconciliation and argued that the unique circumstances of the Vietnam War made a blanket amnesty appropriate. Especially after President Ford's pardon of Richard Nixon on 8 September 1974, amnesty proponents raised questions about the equality of American justice. Opponents claimed that those who violated the law should pay the penalty, and to implicitly approve of their actions degraded the sacrifices and commitment of those who served in the war. President Ford's actions pleased neither side. He created a Clemency Board to allow draft evaders and deserters an "earned amnesty" that required two years of alternative service. Only a small percentage of those eligible applied for clemency, and hiring opportunities proved difficult to find. Most participants in the earned amnesty program eventually received pardons after six months of service. President **Jimmy Carter** later granted a blanket pardon rather than an amnesty to draft resisters, but excluded deserters.

The conflated categories of Americans who were POW and missing in action (MIA) emerged as a second divisive postwar issue. Support for POWs crossed ideological lines and antiwar activists often served as a conduit for returning prisoners before the war ended. The National League of Families of American Prisoners and Missing in Southeast Asia formed in 1967 to advocate for better conditions on behalf of their relatives. In an unprecedented move, the Nixon administration initially attempted to manipulate the POW/MIA issue for its own purposes, and raised the point of accounting for MIAs as a means of extending public support for the war. In the postwar years, prowar forces led by the National League argued that many MIAs actually remained as prisoners in Indochina, an unsubstantiated claim but one pushed by conspiracy theorists and supported by high-profile Hollywood films in the early 1980s such as *Uncommon Valor, Missing in Action*, and *Rambo*. The impact of these spurious claims were evident in the ubiquitous black and white POW/MIA flags and an August 1991 poll that revealed a significant majority of Americans (69 percent) believed US POWs remained in Indochina.

The issue persisted even though the fewer than 2,500 Vietnam-era MIAs represented a much smaller number than in previous wars. Genuinely concerned citizens and political opportunists alike lobbied for a full accounting of American MIAs before considering renewing normal relations with Vietnam. Numerous government investigations also failed to uncover evidence that Americans remained captive in Vietnam. For example, the US Senate Select Committee on POW/MIA Affairs, operating from August 1991 to January 1993, found "no compelling evidence that proves that any American remains alive in captivity in Southeast Asia." Critics of the MIA lobby argue that the charges are politically motivated, and point out that the Vietnamese lost 300,000 of their own MIAs.

Vietnam was important to the United States because its containment policy viewed Vietnam as the key to Southeast Asia. Vietnam by itself was not the threat, but if the domino theory was true, then its control by a communist regime threatened all of Southeast Asia. The loss of that area threatened the economic needs of the Western alliance and Japan. Having learned the lessons of appeasing totalitarian states from World War II, American leaders assumed the worst-case scenario. Containment was designed to avoid repeating that earlier mistake, and Americans believed that Vietnam's attempt to gain independence fit the pattern of communist aggression. Later, as the Americans poured more resources into Vietnam, it became harder to leave. A larger commitment meant avoiding withdrawal and its accompanying loss of prestige. Escalation, however, placed greater emphasis on the US's credibility, threatening its status and international confidence in American power. When the war was over, the impact of defeat in Vietnam was less drastic than some Americans had feared. No dominoes fell outside Indochina.

By viewing Vietnam's struggle for liberation in narrow Cold War terms, the United States mistakenly attributed its local origins to international communism. Entry into the Vietnam War based on this mistaken perception proved to be a very costly endeavor. The price tag is easiest to tally, costing the United States an estimated $167 billion and stimulating inflation at home. Of more lasting significance, however, is the impact of the war on how Americans view themselves and their country. The war stood at the heart of a series of social upheavals that contributed to a growing national discontent with some of its most esteemed institutions, including the government itself. Vietnam also caused Americans to question some of their most fundamental beliefs regarding the nation's benevolence and restraint in using its power.

Vietnam broke the Cold War consensus on foreign policy. The public became preoccupied with domestic crises and less supportive of military intervention around the globe. By the late 1970s the Vietnam debate began to reappear, though few embraced a rapid change. The Carter administration eased the US position against Vietnam, but misunderstandings over Nixon's promises of reconstruction aid prevented reconciliation in 1977. When Hanoi proposed normalization the following year, Carter had shifted to a harder line.

In the 1980s the failure of *détente* and a renewed nationalism brought a return to aggressive foreign policy and massive defense expenditures during the administration of President **Ronald Reagan**. Conservative Republicans were not interested in extending friendly recognition to Vietnam either. The foreign policy debates of the 1980s inevitably included comparisons to Vietnam, which Reagan referred to as "a noble war." Liberals, concerned about misguided commitments in Central America, warned of another Vietnam, while conservatives who advocated stronger positions against communism complained that the Vietnam Syndrome had weakened America's will. Despite President **George H.W. Bush**'s claim, victory in the 1991 Persian Gulf War did not end this influence. Debates over intervention in various parts of the world continue to invoke the specter of Vietnam.

The United States finally moved to mend the relationship with Vietnam under the administration of President **Bill Clinton**. Elected in 1992, Clinton lifted the trade embargo in February 1994 and normalized relations in 1995.

Impact on Vietnam

Pham Van Dong underscored Vietnam's difficult transformation to a unified independent nation with his observation that "Waging a war is simple, but running a country is very difficult" (Karnow, 1983: 9). The war had driven much of the rural population into the cities and destroyed a substantial amount of the best agricultural land. The withdrawal of American support contributed to Vietnam's social and economic problems. Hoping to replace that loss, Vietnam approached the United States about normalizing diplomatic relations in 1977 during the Carter administration. The Vietnamese demand for Nixon's promised reparations, however, brought the talks to an end.

Although Vietnam itself was finally unified, regional and cultural differences and the effects of 30 years of warfare made integration difficult. The South Vietnamese did not suffer the bloodbath predicted by some

Americans, but Hanoi forced perhaps 400,000 of its former opponents to endure as long as ten years in "re-education camps." Many southerners resented what they saw as northern arrogance. Perhaps the major problem of the postwar years was Hanoi's hasty attempt to complete its socialist revolution. Replacing the private southern economy with collectivization in March 1978, combined with high military spending and existing economic problems, made Vietnam one of the world's poorest nations. The social dislocation caused nearly 1.5 million people to flee Vietnam by sea after 1975. Known as the "boat people," they often lived in foreign refugee camps, but almost one million eventually emigrated to the United States.

By the mid-1980s Vietnam's isolation from its Cambodian occupation and declining support from the Soviet Union produced inflation of over 500 percent a year. Following Le Duan's death in 1986, new leadership called for economic reforms moving toward a more open market system and a compromise in Cambodia that would end the economic embargo. The reforms, known as **doi moi**, did achieve some economic growth.

Postwar Debate

The Vietnam War has produced a vast amount of literature covering nearly every aspect of the conflict. Among the central questions that writers have raised are why the United States committed itself to a large military endeavor, and why it failed to achieve its goals. The earliest scholarship took place even as the war escalated during the mid-1960s. The majority of these works, loosely grouped together as the orthodox interpretation, were moderately critical of the American role in Vietnam. George Kahin and John Lewis, in *The United States in Vietnam* (1967), emphasized that US intervention undermined Vietnamese nationalism. A larger group of writers, some of whom were government officials, argued a "quagmire" thesis. This interpretation claimed that misguided idealism and an incomplete understanding of Vietnamese culture and politics motivated the United States. This resulted in the nation being pulled incrementally and against its will into a military situation that it could not win. Some of the best-known works that take this view are David Halberstam's *The Making of a Quagmire* (1964), Arthur Schlesinger Jr.'s *The Bitter Heritage* (1966), and Chester Cooper's *The Lost Crusade* (1970).

Challenges to the quagmire theory's assumption that government leaders were unaware of the implications of their decisions came with the wealth of primary documents available with the publication of *The Pentagon Papers*. In his *Papers on the War* (1972), Daniel Ellsberg argued that American leaders understood that each new escalation on their part would fail to achieve their goals, and that they lied to the public about the war's progress. Leslie Gelb and Richard Betts followed with *The Irony of Vietnam* (1978), claiming that each administration knew of Vietnam's inherent problems and did the minimum necessary to avoid defeat, deliberately choosing actions that would produce a stalemate. This policy succeeded until public support for the war disappeared. Most of these works are critical of American involvement in Vietnam.

The orthodox interpretation grew into the dominant scholarly view of the war. Moving beyond the now discredited quagmire theory, scholars viewed the war as a tragic mistake, with US decision makers supporting a deeply flawed ally with an inappropriate military strategy that was almost certain to fail. The early benchmark for the orthodox interpretation was George C. Herring's *America's Longest War* (1979), but other broad surveys followed. These include Paul Kattenburg, *The Vietnam Trauma in American Foreign Policy* (1980); Stanley Karnow, *Vietnam: A History* (1983), *Vietnam: An American Ordeal* (1990) by George Donelson Moss; Marilyn Young, *The Vietnam Wars* (1991); *Where the Domino Fell* (1991) by James Olson and Randy Roberts; and Robert Schulzinger, *A Time For War* (1997). Loren Baritz's *Backfire* (1985) and James Gibson's *The Perfect War* (1986) emphasize that the United States relied too heavily on technology to win the war rather than trying to understand the unique situation in Vietnam.

These and many other more focused works established a consensus on several key questions on the war. Cold War pressures pushed the United States into a misguided commitment where South Vietnamese and US flaws combined with North Vietnamese and National Liberation Front advantages to produce the eventual outcome. Communist-led forces successfully portrayed themselves as the legitimate defenders of national independence, while South Vietnam represented the colonial past and faced nearly insurmountable internal divisions and problems. Viewing international communism as a monolithic bloc prevented an accurate assessment of regional national aspirations. Despite their concerns regarding South Vietnam's long-term viability, US leaders possessed great faith in the nation's military abilities and were apprehensive about the political implications of not making a stand. The United States failed largely because it sought a military solution to a predominantly political problem, pursuing a war it knew was of peripheral importance primarily to maintain its credibility. South Vietnamese and US forces used a conventional military strategy against an enemy that planned for a protracted war, alternating guerrilla and conventional warfare as the conditions shifted.

Revisionist works generally defended US involvement as a necessary action and believe a more effective use of military power could have won the war. Many blame America's failure on some combination of a critical news media, the antiwar movement, and indecisive politicians. Among the first serious revisionist accounts is Guenter Lewy's *America in Vietnam* (1978). Lewy defends the morality of US objectives and disputes charges that American troops were guilty of war crimes. Norman Pod-horetz's *Why We Were in Vietnam* (1982) and Michael Lind's *Vietnam: The Necessary War* (1999) defend US involvement though they question whether or not the war was winnable.

Several former military officers joined the revisionist ranks. Most blame civilians for placing restraints on the military, which prevented the armed forces from fighting a successful conventional war. William Westmoreland's *A Soldier Reports* (1976) and U.S. Grant Sharp's *Strategy for Defeat* (1978) especially criticize a civilian-imposed policy of graduated escalation for causing America's military defeat, a position echoed in Dave Richard Palmer's *Summons of the Trumpet* (1978). A rapid overwhelming use of force, they argue, would have succeeded. The government's gradual escalation policy allowed the enemy to adjust, and encouraged a domestic antiwar movement that was exacerbated by a biased media. Even with these faults, the military could have won the war had civilians not placed so many restraints upon it, limiting bombing targets, and prohibiting invasions of the North, Cambodia, and Laos. They claim Nixon's removal of many restrictions allowed Vietnamization to succeed, but Congress withdrew its support of South Vietnam and allowed it to collapse in 1975. This view that the military was prevented from winning the war by civilian leadership, the antiwar movement, and the press is known as the stab-in-the-back thesis. Its advocates seek to redeem the US image of nobility and power. If America possessed such great power, they contend, it must have been defeated from within. Some further claim that military victory was not only possible, but would have successfully resolved political issues as well. Despite their focus on civilians, some works do recognize military problems as well.

Harry Summers's *On Strategy* (1982) and Bruce Palmer Jr.'s *The 25-Year War* (1984) criticize both civilian and military strategy. Summers argues that Westmoreland's search and destroy strategy wasted manpower by emphasizing counterinsurgency. A conventional war waged against North Vietnam could have brought victory. Palmer arrives at a similar conclusion. Other books, such as Shelby Stanton's *The Rise and Fall of an American Army* (1985) and Phillip Davidson's *Vietnam at War* (1988), similarly criticize civilian decisions and argue that the war was winnable, but also contend that Westmoreland's search and destroy strategy deserves blame as well. Stanton contradicts Summers and argues that the war was waged in a conventional manner, but should have been fought as a counterinsurgency.

Another group of revisionists generally accepts the possibility of victory, but emphasizes military rather than civilian mistakes. Andrew Krepinevich's *The Army and Vietnam* (1986), David Hackworth's *About Face* (1989), William Colby's *Lost Victory* (1989), Larry Cable's *Unholy Grail* (1991), and Lewis Sorley's *A Better War* (1999) all maintain that the military's emphasis on fighting a conventional war through a search and destroy strategy was ineffective. They argue to varying degrees that greater emphasis on counterinsurgency might have brought victory. Some of these criticize General Westmoreland for not understanding guerrilla warfare.

The most noteworthy recent example of revisionist scholarship is Mark Moyar, *Triumph Forsaken* (2006). A synthesis of US involvement in Vietnam up through 1965, this work argues that Ho Chi Minh's dedicated Marxism demanded an American military response to prevent a series of falling dominoes. Further, Moyar claims that Ngo Dinh Diem led South Vietnam effectively and that the US–South Vietnamese alliance was succeeding on the battlefield until his ill-conceived overthrow in 1963. Moyar blames inaccurate news reports for persuading both the public and key officials that the Saigon regime was both politically and militarily unstable.

Orthodox historians have effectively refuted most revisionist claims. James Thompson's *Rolling Thunder* (1980), Mark Clodfelter's *The Limits of Air Power* (1989), Earl Tilford Jr.'s *Crosswinds* (1993), and Ronald Frankum Jr.'s *Like Rolling Thunder* (2005) all detail the limitations of the US bombing campaigns. Daniel Hallin, *The Uncensored War* (1986), William Hammond, *Reporting Vietnam* (1998), and Clarence Wyatt, *Paper Soldiers* (1993) effectively refuted the claim that the media created wartime dissent. Kevin Boylan, *Losing Binh Dinh* (2016), is a careful study of a key province that persuasively undermines revisionist arguments that the United States had effectively won the war because of South Vietnam's successful pacification. Among other noteworthy books, Fredrik Logevall, *Choosing War* (1999), claims that President Johnson had viable options to military escalation but engaged for largely political reasons. Mark Bradley, *Imagining Vietnam and America* (2000), argues that Vietnamese communist and American decisions grew more out of their perceptions of one another than reality. Seth Jacobs, *America's Miracle Man in Vietnam* (2004), points to the errors that led to US support for Ngo Dinh Diem's unsuccessful rule.

Orthodox scholars have modified a number of arguments over time while maintaining an essentially critical view of American involvement. They generally view US intervention as mistaken and the war as unwinnable. These writers give greater attention to Vietnamese circumstances rather than American weaknesses in explaining the war's outcome. The Saigon government lacked the legitimacy of the communist-led nationalist movement, and the South's chronic instability handicapped US efforts to prevail. American leaders never understood the commitment of Hanoi to reunification. This "post-revisionist" interpretation is evident in the updated editions of *America's Longest War* (2014) by George Herring, *Vietnam: An American Ordeal* (2010) by George Donelson Moss and *Where the Domino Fell* (2013) by James Olson and Randy Roberts, and in David Anderson, *The Vietnam War* (2005). All of these view the

Vietnam conflict within the context of the Cold War. United States intervention was an effort to preserve a noncommunist state in South Vietnam. The war reflected a misapplication of the containment policy based on a misunderstanding of Vietnam's circumstances.

The orthodox interpretation dominates current scholarship, particularly among professional historians. Orthodoxy effectively refutes the view that the US defeat came from American politicians whose restrictions undermined military success or from an unappreciative public. Every American war occurred with civilian oversight and limitations on military actions. Military leaders provided most of the information used by decision makers, some of it dangerously misleading. In reality, the US armed forces had wide latitude in developing a strategy to achieve its goals.

The military failed to utilize an effective strategy against the Vietnamese communists. It tried to impose its conventional style upon a largely guerrilla situation, fighting a war of attrition instead of providing security to peasants. United States pacification efforts came too late or with too little emphasis. American tactics remained tied to heavy firepower rather than building better relationships at the village level. Despite this evidence, the myth of the stab-in-the-back thesis enjoys some popularity through books and films.

Conclusion

The Viet Minh's victory over the French in 1954 validated their nationalist credentials for most other Vietnamese. Their control of a more unified region in the North enhanced the long-term struggle for unification and independence. By comparison, South Vietnam suffered poor leadership, lacked broad appeal to its citizens, and was far too dependent upon the Americans. Because of the Cold War, the United States tried to build a nation in the South, and it became a test of its credibility. American officials, but especially Presidents Johnson and Nixon, recognized the difficulty of winning, but the Cold War and credibility made it difficult to turn away. Americans wanted to end the war, but they also wanted to win. Not until the United States was willing to relinquish significant political influence to the National Liberation Front and the communists agreed to leave Thieu in power did negotiations produce an acceptable compromise. The 1973 agreement acted only as a short cease-fire. The war quickly renewed and escalated dramatically in the winter of 1974–1975. South Vietnamese society collapsed as the North completed the Vietnamese revolution.

In the long run Vietnam turned out not to be as significant to US national security as first believed. The consequences of defeat were much smaller than Americans had feared. At the same time, victory for the North Vietnamese marked a new beginning rather than the attainment of Vietnam's acceptance into the community of nations. The struggle for economic and social stability continues.

If one phrase encapsulates Vietnam's determination to prevail against remarkable odds, it would be Ho Chi Minh's 1946 warning directed at the French prime minister. It could as easily have been addressed to the Americans. "If we must fight, we will fight," he promised. "You will kill ten of our men, and we will kill one of yours. Yet, in the end, it is you who will tire."

Part 3

Documents

Document 1

The Quagmire Theory of the Vietnam War

Arthur Schlesinger, Jr. argues that the United States moved unsuspectingly into war through a series of small steps that promised success but ultimately failed.

Things became so desperate in the early months of 1965 . . . that only the February decision to start bombing the north, followed by the commitment of American combat forces the next month, averted total collapse . . . The number of American troops doubled, and doubled again. . . . The bombing steadily grew. . . . As we increased our activity, Hanoi reciprocated . . .

And so the policy of "one more step" lured the United States deeper and deeper into the morass. In retrospect, Vietnam is a triumph of the politics of inadvertence. We have achieved our present entanglement, not after due and deliberate consideration, but through a series of small decisions. It is not only idle but unfair to seek out guilty men. President Eisenhower, after rejecting American military intervention in 1954, set in motion the policy of support for Saigon which resulted, two presidents later, in American military intervention in 1965. Each step in the deepening of the American commitment was reasonably regarded at the time as the last that would be necessary. Yet, in retrospect, each step led only to the next, until we find ourselves entrapped today in that nightmare of American strategists, a land war in Asia – a war which no President, including President Johnson, desired or intended. The Vietnam story is a tragedy without villains . . .

> Source: Arthur M. Schlesinger, Jr., *The Bitter Heritage: Vietnam and American Democracy, 1941–1966* (Boston, MA: Houghton Mifflin, 1966), pp. 46–48.

Document 2

A Revisionist View of the Vietnam War

Mark Moyar argues that the United States was correct to defend South Vietnam and could have prevailed by using different policies.

In sum, South Vietnam was a vital interest of the United States during the period from 1954 to 1965. The aggressive expansionism of North Vietnam and China threatened South Vietnam's existence, and by 1965 only strong American action could keep South Vietnam out of Communist hands. America's policy of defending South Vietnam was therefore sound. US intervention in Vietnam was not an act of strategic buffoonery, nor was it a sinister, warmongering plot that should forever stand as a terrible blemish on America's soul. Neither was it an act of hubris in which the United States pursued objectives far beyond its means. Where the United States erred seriously was in formulating its strategies for protecting South Vietnam. The most terrible mistake was the inciting of the November 1963 coup, for Ngo Dinh Diem's overthrow forfeited the tremendous gains of the preceding nine years and plunged the country into an extended period of instability and weakness. The Johnson administration was handed the thorny tasks of handling the post-coup mess and defending South Vietnam against an increasingly ambitious enemy—and in neither case did the administration achieve good results. President Johnson had available several aggressive policy options that could have enabled South Vietnam to continue the war either without the help of any American ground forces at all or with the employment of US ground forces in advantageous positions outside South Vietnam. But Johnson ruled out these options and therefore, during the summer of 1965, he would have to fight a defensive war within South Vietnam's borders in order to avoid the dreadful international consequences of abandoning the country.

> Source: Mark Moyar, *Triumph Forsaken: The Vietnam War,*
> *1954–1965* (Cambridge, UK: Cambridge University
> Press, 2006), pp. xxii–xxiii.

Document 3

An Orthodox, Post-Revisionist View of the Vietnam War

George Herring presents an orthodox, post-revisionist interpretation of the Vietnam War.

The U.S. war in Vietnam was a logical, if by no means inevitable, outgrowth of its Cold War world view and the policy of containment that Americans in and out of government accepted without serious question for more than two decades. The concept of containment of Communist expansion provided the broad parameters in which the Vietnam commitment took shape. Some writers have argued that the dictates of the Cold War consensus were so compelling that policymakers had little choice but to follow where they led. Recent scholarship has challenged this view. At each step on the long road to war alternatives were presented and discussed; choices were available. That presidents chose escalation was not primarily a result of blind obeisance to the dictates of ideology . . .

I still believe that U.S. intervention in Vietnam was misguided. It can be argued that the containment policy worked in Europe, contributing significantly, maybe even decisively, to the outcome of the Cold War. That said, I am persuaded that containment was misapplied in Vietnam.

Obsessed with their determination to stop the advance of communism, and abysmally ignorant of the Vietnamese people and their history, Americans profoundly misread the nature of the struggle in Vietnam, its significance for their vital interests, and its susceptibility to their influence.

Defeat came hard, and in its aftermath it has been fashionable for many Americans to argue that victory could have been attained if the United States had only fought the war more decisively or in a different way. Such views are perhaps comforting for a people spoiled by success. They accord with what the English scholar D.W. Brogan once called "the illusion of American omnipotence," the belief, almost an article of faith among Americans, that this nation can do anything it sets its mind to. The enduring "lesson" of the Vietnam War is that power, no matter how great, has limits. American power in Vietnam was constrained by the Cold War, in whose name, ironically, it was fought. It was limited by the weakness of America's client, South Vietnam, and by the determination and willingness of its foes—North Vietnam and the National Liberation Front of South Vietnam—to pay any price. Given these circumstances, I do not believe that the war could have been won in any meaningful sense or at a moral or a material price Americans would—or should—have been willing to pay.

Source: George C. Herring, *America's Longest War: The United States and Vietnam, 1950–1975*, 5th edition (New York: McGraw-Hill, 2014), pp. xii–xiii.

Document 4

Roosevelt's Memo to Secretary of State Cordell Hull, 24 January 1944

President Franklin Roosevelt favored a postwar trusteeship system for colonial possessions, but ultimately conceded to his British and French allies.

I saw Halifax [Lord Halifax, the British ambassador to the United States] last week and told him quite frankly that it was perfectly true that I had, for over a year, expressed the opinion that Indo-China should not go back to France but that it should be administered by an international trusteeship. France has had the country – thirty million inhabitants for nearly one hundred years, and the people are worse off than they were at the beginning.

As a matter of interest, I am wholeheartedly supported in this view by Generalissimo Chiang Kai-shek and by Marshal Stalin. I see no reason to play in with the British Foreign Office in this matter. The only reason they seem to oppose it is that they fear the effect it would have on their possessions and those of the Dutch. They have never liked the idea of trusteeship because it is, in some instances, aimed at future independence. This is true in the case of Indo-China.

Each case must, of course, stand on its own feet, but the case of Indo-China is perfectly clear. France has milked it for one hundred years. The people of Indo-China are entitled to something better than that.

Source: *United States-Vietnam Relations, 1945–1967*:
Study Prepared by Department of Defense, printed
for the use of House Committee on Armed Services.
Book 1, pp. A–14. Washington, DC: Government
Printing Office, 1971.

Document 5

The Vietnamese Declaration of Independence

The Vietnamese Declaration of Independence, delivered by Ho Chi Minh in Hanoi, 2 September 1945

All men are created equal. They are endowed by their Creator with certain unalienable rights, among these are Life, Liberty, and the pursuit of Happiness.

This immortal statement was made in the Declaration of Independence of the United States of America in 1776. In a broader sense, this means: All the peoples on the earth are equal from birth, all the peoples have a right to live, to be happy and free.

The Declaration of the French Revolution made in 1791 on the Rights of Man and the Citizen also states: "All men are born free and with equal rights, and must always remain free and have equal rights."

Those are undeniable truths.

Nevertheless, for more than eighty years, the French imperialists, abusing the standard of Liberty, Equality, and Fraternity, have violated our Fatherland and oppressed our fellow citizens. They have acted contrary to the ideals of humanity and justice.

In the field of politics, they have deprived our people of every democratic liberty.

They have enforced inhuman laws; they have set up three distinct political regimes in the North, the Center, and the South of Viet Nam in order to wreck our national unity and prevent our people from being united.

They have built more prisons than schools. They have mercilessly slain our patriots; they have drowned our uprisings in rivers of blood.

They have fettered public opinion; they have practiced obscurantism against our people.

To weaken our race they have forced us to use opium and alcohol.

In the field of economics, they have fleeced us to the backbone, impoverished our people, and devastated our land.

They have robbed us of our rice fields, our mines, our forests, and our raw materials. They have monopolized the issuing of bank notes and the export trade.

They have invented numerous unjustifiable taxes and reduced our people, especially our peasantry, to a state of extreme poverty.

They have hampered the prospering of our national bourgeoisie; they have mercilessly exploited our workers.

In the autumn of 1940, when the Japanese fascists violated Indo-China's territory to establish new bases in their fight against the Allies, the French imperialists went down on their bended knees and handed over our country to them.

Thus, from that date, our people were subjected to the double yoke of the French and the Japanese. Their sufferings and miseries increased. The result was that from the end of last year to the beginning of this year, from Quang Tri province to the North of Viet Nam, more than two million of our fellow citizens died from starvation. On the 9th of March [1945], the French troops were disarmed by the Japanese. The French colonialists either fled or surrendered, showing that not only were they incapable of "protecting" us, but that, in the span of five years, they had twice sold our country to the Japanese.

On several occasions before the 9th of March, the Viet Minh League urged the French to ally themselves with it against the Japanese. Instead of agreeing to this proposal, the French colonialists so intensified their terrorist activities against the Viet Minh members that before fleeing they massacred a great number of our political prisoners detained at Yen Bay and Cao Bang.

Notwithstanding all this, our fellow citizens have always manifested toward the French a tolerant and humane attitude. Even after the Japanese putsch of March, 1945, the Viet Minh League helped many Frenchmen to cross the frontier, rescued some of them from Japanese jails, and protected French lives and property.

From the autumn of 1940, our country had in fact ceased to be a French colony and had become a Japanese possession.

After the Japanese had surrendered to the Allies, our whole people rose to regain our national sovereignty and to found the Democratic Republic of Viet Nam.

The truth is that we have wrested our independence from the Japanese and not from the French.

The French have fled, the Japanese have capitulated, Emperor Bao Dai had abdicated. Our people have broken the chains, which for nearly a century have fettered them and have won independence for the Fatherland. Our people at the same time have overthrown the monarchic regime that has reigned supreme for dozens of centuries. In its place has been established the present Democratic Republic.

For these reasons, we, members of the Provisional Government, representing the whole Vietnamese people, declare that from now on we break off all relations of a colonial character with France; we repeal all the international obligation that France has so far subscribed to on behalf of Viet Nam, and we abolish all the special rights the French have unlawfully acquired in our Fatherland.

The whole Vietnamese people, animated by a common purpose, are determined to fight to the bitter end against any attempt by the French colonialists to reconquer their country.

We are convinced that the Allied nations, which at Teheran and San Francisco have acknowledged the principles of self-determination and equality of nations, will not refuse to acknowledge the independence of Viet Nam.

A people who have courageously opposed French domination for more than eighty years, a people who have fought side by side with the Allies against the fascists during these last years, such a people must be free and independent.

For these reasons, we, members of the Provisional Government of the Democratic Republic of Viet Nam, solemnly declare to the world that Viet Nam has the right to be a free and independent country – and in fact it is so already. The entire Vietnamese people are determined to mobilize all their physical and mental strength, to sacrifice their lives and property in order to safeguard their independence and liberty.

Source: Ho Chi Minh, *Selected Works*, 4 vols. (Hanoi: Foreign Languages Publishing House, 1960–1962), III, pp. 17–21.

Document 6

Economic and Military Aid Urged for Indochina

Secretary of State Dean Acheson advocates US support for France in the French–Indochina War, 8 May 1950.

The [French] Foreign Minister [Robert Schuman] and I have just had an exchange of views on the situation in Indochina and are in general agreement both as to the urgency of the situation in that area and as to the necessity for remedial action. We have noted the fact that the problem of meeting the threat to the security of Viet Nam, Cambodia, and Laos which now enjoy independence within the French union is primarily the responsibility of France and the Governments and peoples of Indochina. The United States recognizes that the solution of the Indochina problem depends both upon the restoration of security and upon the development of genuine nationalism and that United States assistance can and should contribute to these major objectives. The United States Government, convinced that neither national independence nor democratic evolution exist in any area dominated by Soviet imperialism, considers the situation to be such as to warrant its according economic aid and military equipment to the associated states of Indochina and to France in order to assist them in restoring stability and permitting these states to pursue their peaceful and democratic development.

Source: *US Department of State Bulletin*, vol. 22
(22 May 1950), p. 821.

Document 7

The Domino Theory, April 1954

During a press conference on 7 April 1954, President Dwight Eisenhower references the domino theory.

Q. Robert Richards, Copley Press: Mr. President, would you mind commenting on the strategic importance of Indochina to the free world? I think there has been, across the country, some lack of understanding on just what it means to us.

The President: You have, of course, both the specific and the general when you talk about such things.

First of all, you have the specific value of a locality in its production of materials that the world needs.

Then you have the possibility that many human beings pass under a dictatorship that is inimical to the free world.

Finally, you have broader considerations that might follow what you would call the "falling domino" principle. You have a row of dominoes set up, you knock over the first one, and what will happen to the last one is the certainty that it will go over very quickly. So you could have a beginning of a disintegration that would have the most profound influences.

Now, with respect to the first one, two of the items from this particular area that the world uses are tin and tungsten. They are very important. There are others, of course, the rubber plantations and so on.

Then with respect to more people passing under this domination, Asia, after all, has already lost some 450 million of its peoples to the Communist dictatorship, and we simply can't afford greater losses.

But when we come to the possible sequence of events, the loss of Indochina, of Burma, of Thailand, of the Peninsula, and Indonesia following, now you begin to talk about areas that not only multiply the disadvantages that you would suffer through loss of materials, sources of materials, but now you are talking really about millions and millions and millions of people.

Finally, the geographical position achieved thereby does many things. It turns the so-called island defensive chain of Japan, Formosa, of the Philippines and to the southward; it moves in to threaten Australia and New Zealand.

It takes away, in its economic aspects, that region that Japan must have as a trading area or Japan, in turn, will have only one place in the world to go—that is, toward the Communist areas in order to live.

So, the possible consequences of the loss are just incalculable to the free world.

Source: *Public Papers of the Presidents of the United States: Dwight D. Eisenhower, 1954* (Washington, DC: Government Printing Office, 1958), pp. 382–383.

Document 8

The Geneva Accords, 1954

The Final Declaration of the Geneva Conference on Indochina, 21 July 1954

1. The Conference takes note of the agreements ending hostilities in Cambodia, Laos, and Vietnam and organizing international control and the supervision of the execution of the provisions of these agreements.
2. The Conference expresses satisfaction at the end of hostilities in Cambodia, Laos, and Vietnam; the Conference expresses its conviction that the execution of the provisions set out in the present declaration and in the agreements of the cessation of hostilities will permit Cambodia, Laos, and Vietnam henceforth to play their part, in full independence and sovereignty, in the peaceful community of nations.
3. The Conference takes note of the declarations made by the Governments of Cambodia and Laos of their intention to adopt measures permitting all citizens to take their place in the national community, in particular by participating in the next general elections, which, in conformity with the constitution of each of these countries, shall take place in the course of the year 1955, by secret ballot and in conditions of respect for fundamental freedoms.
4. The Conference takes note of the clauses in the agreement on the cessation of hostilities in Vietnam prohibiting the introduction into Vietnam of foreign troops and military personnel as well as of all kinds of arms and munitions. The Conference also takes note of the declarations made by the Governments of Cambodia and Laos of their resolution not to request foreign aid, whether in war material, in personnel, or in instructors except for the purpose of the effective defense of their territory and, in the case of Laos, to the extent defined by the agreements of the cessation of hostilities in Laos.

5. The Conference takes note of the clause in the agreement on the cessation of hostilities in Vietnam to the effect that no military base under the control of a foreign State may be established in the regrouping zones of the two parties, the latter having the obligation to see that the zones allotted to them shall not constitute part of any military alliance and shall not be utilized for the resumption of hostilities or in the service of an aggressive policy. The Conference also takes note of the declarations of the Governments of Cambodia and Laos to the effect that they will not join in any agreement with other States if this agreement includes the obligation to participate in a military alliance not in conformity with the principles of the Charter of the United Nations or, in the case of Laos, with the principles of the agreement on the cessation of hostilities in Laos or, so long as their security is not threatened, the obligation to establish bases on Cambodian or Laotian territory for the military forces of foreign powers.

6. The Conference recognizes that the essential purpose of the agreement relating to Vietnam is to settle military questions with a view to ending hostilities and that the military demarcation line is provisional and should not in any way be interpreted as constituting a political or territorial boundary. The Conference expresses its conviction that the execution of the provisions set out in the present declaration and in the agreement on the cessation of hostilities creates the necessary basis for the achievement in the near future of a political settlement in Vietnam.

7. The Conference declares that, so far as Vietnam is concerned, the settlement of political problems, effected on the basis of respect for the principles of independence, unity, and territorial integrity, shall permit the Vietnamese people to enjoy the fundamental freedoms, guaranteed by democratic institutions established as a result of free general elections by secret ballot. In order to ensure that sufficient progress in the restoration of peace has been made, and that all the necessary conditions obtain for free expression of the national will, general elections shall be held in July 1956 under the supervision of an international commission composed of representatives of the Member States of the International Supervisory Commission, referred to in the agreement on the cessation of hostilities. Consultations will be held on this subject between the competent representative authorities of the two zones from July 20, 1955, onward.

8. The provisions of the agreements on the cessation of hostilities intended to ensure the protection of individuals and of property must be most strictly applied and must, in particular, allow everyone in Vietnam to decide freely in which zone he wishes to live.

9. The competent representative authorities of the North and South zones of Vietnam, as well as the authorities of Laos and Cambodia, must not permit any individual or collective reprisals against persons who had collaborated in any way with one of the parties during the war, or against members of such persons' families.

10. The Conference takes note of the declaration of the Government of the French Republic to the effect that it is ready to withdraw its troops from the territory of Cambodia, Laos, and Vietnam, at the request of the Governments concerned and within periods which shall be fixed by agreement between the parties except in the cases where, by agreement between the two parties, a certain number of French troops shall remain at specified points and for a specified time.

11. The Conference takes note of the declaration of the French Government to the effect that for the settlement of all the problems connected with the re-establishment and consolidation of peace in Cambodia, Laos, and Vietnam, the French Government will proceed from the principle of respect for the independence and sovereignty, unity and territorial integrity of Cambodia, Laos, and Vietnam.

12. In their relations with Cambodia, Laos, and Vietnam, each member of the Geneva Conference undertakes to respect the sovereignty, the independence, the unity, and the territorial integrity of the above-mentioned States, and to refrain from any interference in their internal affairs.

13. The members of the Conference agree to consult one another on any question which may be referred to them by the International Supervisory Commission, in order to study such measures as may prove necessary to ensure that the agreements on the cessation of hostilities in Cambodia, Laos, and Vietnam are respected.

> Source: *The Pentagon Papers: The Defense Department History of Decisionmaking on Vietnam*, The Senator Gravel edition, 5 vols. (Boston: Beacon Press, 1971–72), I, pp. 279–282, reprinted in Spencer C. Tucker (ed.), *Encyclopedia of the Vietnam War: A Political, Social, and Military History*, 3 vols. (Santa Barbara, CA: ABC–CLIO, 1998), pp. 934–935.

Document 9

The Tonkin Gulf Resolution

Passed by the US Congress on 7 August 1964 in response to naval engagements between US and North Vietnamese forces in the Gulf of Tonkin

Whereas naval units of the Communist regime in Vietnam, in violation of the principles of the Charter of the United Nations and of international law, have deliberately and repeatedly attacked United States naval vessels lawfully present in international waters, and have thereby created a serious threat to international peace; and

Whereas these attacks are part of a deliberate and systematic campaign of aggression that the Communist regime in North Vietnam has been waging against its neighbors and the nations joined with them in the collective defense of their freedom; and

Whereas the United States is assisting the peoples of southeast Asia to protect their freedom and has no territorial, military or political ambitions in that area, but desires only that these peoples should be left in peace to work out their own destinies in their own way: Now, therefore, be it.

Resolved by the Senate and House of Representatives of the United States of America in Congress assembled, That the Congress approves and supports the determination of the President, as Commander in Chief, to take all necessary measures to repel any armed attack against the forces of the United States and to prevent further aggression.

SEC. 2. The United States regards as vital to its national interest and to world peace the maintenance of international peace and security in southeast Asia. Consonant with the Constitution of the United States and the Charter of the United Nations and in accordance with its obligations under the Southeast Asia Collective Defense Treaty, the United States is, therefore, prepared, as the President determines, to take all necessary steps, including the use of armed force, to assist any member or protocol state of the Southeast Asia Collective Defense Treaty requesting assistance in defense of its freedom.

SEC. 3. This resolution shall expire when the President shall determine that the peace and security of the area is reasonably assured by international conditions created by action of the United Nations or otherwise, except that it may be terminated earlier by concurrent resolution of the Congress.

Source: *US Department of State Bulletin*, vol. 51,
no. 1313 (24 August 1964), p. 268.

Document 10

"Aggression from the North"

The US State Department released this White Paper on 27 February 1965 as a rationale for American involvement in Vietnam.

South Viet-Nam is fighting for its life against a brutal campaign of terror and armed attack inspired, directed, supplied, and controlled by the Communist regime in Hanoi. This flagrant aggression has been going on for years, but recently the pace has quickened and the threat has now become acute . . .

In Viet-Nam a Communist government has set out deliberately to conquer a sovereign people in a neighboring state. And to achieve its end, it has used every resource of its own government to carry out its carefully planned program of concealed aggression. North Viet-Nam's commitment to seize control of the South is no less total than was the commitment of the regime in North Korea in 1950. But knowing the consequences of the latter's undisguised attack, the planners in Hanoi have tried desperately to conceal their hand. They have failed and their aggression is as real as that of an invading army ...

The evidence shows that the hard core of the Communist forces attacking South Viet-Nam were trained in the North and ordered into the South by Hanoi. It shows that the key leadership of the Viet-Cong (VC), the officers and much of the cadre, many of the technicians, political organizers, and propagandists have come from the North and operate under Hanoi's direction. It shows that the training of essential military personnel and their infiltration into the South is directed by the Military High Command in Hanoi.

Source: US Department of State Bulletin, vol. 52,
no. 1343 (22 March 1965), pp. 404–427.

Document 11

Hanoi's Negotiating Position

Following President Johnson's Johns Hopkins speech, which offered to open peace discussions, North Vietnam responded with these four negotiating points on 8 April 1965.

The unswerving policy of the DRV Government is to respect strictly the 1954 Geneva agreements on Vietnam and to implement correctly their basic provisions as embodied in the following points:

1. Recognition of the basic national rights of the Vietnamese people – peace, independence, sovereignty, unity and territorial integrity. According to the Geneva Agreements, the US Government must withdraw from South Vietnam all US troops, military personnel and weapons of all kinds, dismantle all US military bases there, and cancel its military alliance with South Vietnam. According to the Geneva Agreements, the US Government must stop its acts of war against North Vietnam and completely cease all encroachments on the territory and sovereignty of the DRV.

2. Pending the peaceful reunification of Vietnam, while Vietnam is still temporarily divided into two zones the military provisions of the 1954 Geneva agreements on Vietnam must be strictly respected. The

two zones must refrain from entering into any military alliance with foreign countries and there must be no foreign military bases, troops, or military personnel in their respective territory.

3. The internal affairs of South Vietnam must be settled by the South Vietnamese people themselves in accordance with the program of the National Liberation Front of South Vietnam without any foreign interference.

4. The peaceful reunification of Vietnam is to be settled by the Vietnamese people in both zones, without any foreign interference.

This stand of the DRV Government unquestionably enjoys the approval and support of all peace- and justice-loving governments and peoples in the world. The government of the DRV is of the view that the stand expounded here is the basis for the soundest political settlement of the Vietnam problem.

Source: Pham Van Dong, *Pham Van Dong: Selected Writings*,
pp. 90–158, reprinted in Spencer C. Tucker (ed.),
Encyclopedia of the Vietnam War
(Santa Barbara, CA: ABC–CLIO, 1998) p. 1004.

Document 12

"A Compromise Solution in South Vietnam"

Undersecretary of State George Ball, in this 1 July 1965 memorandum to President Lyndon Johnson, warned against an American military escalation.

The South Vietnamese are losing the war to the Viet Cong. No one can assure you that we can beat the Viet Cong or even force them to the conference table on our terms, no matter how many hundred thousand white, foreign (US) troops we deploy . . .

The Question to Decide: Should we limit our liabilities in South Vietnam and try to find a way out with minimal long-term costs?

The alternative – no matter what we may wish it to be – is almost certainly a protracted war involving an open-ended commitment of US forces, mounting US casualties, no assurance of a satisfactory solution, and a serious danger of escalation at the end of the road . . .

So long as our forces are restricted to advising and assisting the South Vietnamese, the struggle will remain a civil war between Asian peoples. Once we deploy substantial numbers of troops in combat it will become a war between the US and a large part of the population of South Vietnam, organized and directed from North Vietnam and backed by the resources of both Moscow and Peiping.

The decision you face now, therefore, is crucial. Once large numbers of US troops are committed to direct combat, they will begin to take heavy casualties in a war they are ill-equipped to fight in a non-cooperative if not downright hostile countryside.

Once we suffer large casualties, we will have started a well-nigh irreversible process. Our involvement will be so great that we cannot – without national humiliation – stop short of achieving our complete objectives. Of the two possibilities I think humiliation would be more likely than the achievement of our objectives – even after we have paid terrible costs . . .

> Source: Neil Sheehan, *The Pentagon Papers as published by the New York Times* (New York: Bantam Books, 1971), pp. 449–454.

Document 13

McNamara Presents Options to President Johnson

Secretary of Defense Robert McNamara's memo of 20 July 1965 recommended military escalation in Vietnam.

4. Options open to us. We must choose among three courses of action with respect to Vietnam all of which involve different probabilities, outcomes and costs:

(a) Cut our losses and withdraw under the best conditions that can be arranged – almost certainly conditions humiliating the United States and very damaging to our future effectiveness on the world scene.

(b) Continue at about the present level, with the US forces limited to say 75,000, holding on and playing for the breaks – a course of action which, because our position would grow weaker, almost certainly would confront us later with a choice between withdrawal and an emergency expansion of forces, perhaps too late to do any good.

(c) Expand promptly and substantially the US military pressure against the Viet Cong in the South and maintain the military pressure against the North Vietnamese in the North while launching a vigorous effort on the political side to lay the groundwork for a favorable outcome by clarifying our objectives and establishing channels of communication. This alternative would stave off defeat in the short run and offer a good chance of producing a favorable settlement in the longer run; at the same time it would imply a commitment to see a fighting war clear through at considerable cost in casualties and material and would make any later decision to withdraw even more difficult and even more costly than would be the case today.

My recommendations in paragraph 5 below are based on the choice of the third alternative (Option c) as the course of action involving the best odds of the best outcome with the most acceptable cost to the United States.

Source: Document from the Lyndon Baines Johnson Library, reprinted in Spencer C. Tucker (ed.), *Encyclopedia of the Vietnam War* (Santa Barbara, CA: ABC–CLIO, 1998) p. 1008.

Document 14

Washington's Negotiating Position

During a pause in the bombing of North Vietnam from Christmas 1965 to 31 January 1966, the United States issued these negotiating points on 7 January 1966.

The following statements are on the public record about elements which the United States believes can go into peace in Southeast Asia:

1. The Geneva Agreements of 1954 and 1962 are an adequate basis for peace in Southeast Asia;
2. We would welcome a conference on Southeast Asia or on any part thereof;
3. We would welcome "negotiations without pre-conditions" as the 17 nations put it;
4. We would welcome unconditional discussions as President Johnson put it;
5. A cessation of hostilities could be the first order of business at a conference or could be the subject of preliminary discussions;
6. Hanoi's four points could be discussed along with other points which others might wish to propose;
7. We want no US bases in Southeast Asia;
8. We do not desire to retain US troops in South Vietnam after peace is assured;
9. We support free elections in South Vietnam to give the South Vietnamese a government of their own choice;
10. The question of reunification of Vietnam should be determined by the Vietnamese through their own free decision;
11. The countries of Southeast Asia can be nonaligned or neutral if that is their option;
12. We would much prefer to use our resources for the economic reconstruction of Southeast Asia than in war. If there is peace, North Vietnam could participate in a regional effort to which we would be prepared to contribute at least one billion dollars;

13. The President has said, "The Vietcong would not have difficulty being represented and having their views represented if for a moment Hanoi decided she wanted to cease aggression. I don't think that would be an unsurmountable problem."
14. We have said publicly and privately that we could stop the bombing of North Vietnam as a step toward peace although there has not been the slightest hint or suggestion from the other side as to what they would do if the bombing stopped.

Source: *US Department of State Bulletin*, vol. 54,
no. 1390 (14 February 1966), p. 225.

Document 15

Letter from Ho Chi Minh to Lyndon Johnson

This letter of 15 February 1967 responded to President Johnson's 8 February letter proposing negotiations between the United States and North Vietnam.

Vietnam is thousands of miles away from the United States. The Vietnamese people have never done any harm to the United States. But contrary to the pledges made by its representative at the 1954 Geneva Conference, the US Government has ceaselessly intervened in Vietnam, it has unleashed and intensified the war of aggression in South Vietnam with a view to prolonging the partition of Vietnam and turning South Vietnam into a neo-colony and a military base of the United States. For over two years now, the US Government has, with its air and naval forces, carried the war to the Democratic Republic of Vietnam, an independent and sovereign country . . .

The Vietnamese people deeply love independence, freedom and peace. But in the face of the US aggression, they have risen up, united as one man, fearless of sacrifices and hardships; they are determined to carry on their Resistance until they have won genuine independence and freedom and true peace. Our just cause enjoys strong sympathy and support from the peoples of the whole world including broad sections of the American people.

The US Government has unleashed the war of aggression in Vietnam. It must cease this aggression. That is the only way to the restoration of peace. The US Government must stop definitively and unconditionally its bombing raids and all others acts of war against the Democratic Republic of Vietnam, withdraw from South Vietnam all US and satellite troops, recognize the South Vietnam National Front for Liberation, and let the Vietnamese people settle themselves their own affairs . . .

The Vietnamese people will never submit to force; they will never accept talks under the threat of bombs.

Our cause is absolutely just. It is to be hoped that the US Government will act in accordance with reason.

Sincerely,

Ho Chi Minh

Source: "Ho Chi Minh's Reply to Lyndon B. Johnson, 15 February 1967," *President Ho Chi Minh Answers President L.B. Johnson*, reprinted in Steven Cohen (ed.), *Vietnam: Anthology and Guide to a Television History* (New York: Alfred A. Knopf, 1983), pp. 147–148.

Document 16

CIA Analysis of the Anti-Vietnam War Movement

This report provided the CIA's assessment of the American antiwar movement in October 1967.

1. The Peace Movement: Confusion, Coordination, and Communism

1. The American peace "movement" is not one but many movements; and the groups involved are as varied as they are numerous. The most striking single characteristic of the peace front is its diversity . . .
3. One thing brings them all together: their opposition to US actions in Vietnam. They do not join up for the same reasons, of course; there are as many motives as there are groups. And they function on different levels: some motives are politically inspired and professional while others are purely personal, some are focused on Vietnam exclusively while others are related to the war only incidentally.
4. One explanation for the diversity of motivation and outlook is the fact that the anti-war sentiment has taken root in separate sectors of the society having little else in common. In addition to the professional pacifists, activists come from the student world, from militant elements of the Negro and other minority communities, from the labor movement, and from the intellectual sphere. In some cases – the civil rights and labor movements specifically – the rank and file are largely disinterested in international problems. But their leaders may not be; some are as active as the intellectual and student leaders both at home and abroad. Each projects his own personal attitudes and prejudices, which frequently are not representative of the group he speaks for . . .

6. Out of such diversity comes much confusion and more than a little disagreement. Strains are evident both on the home front and in their international activities. The job of coordinating a program of joint action, first within the US and then internationally, is an enormous one. Given the strains and complications involved, the performance of the coordinators is impressive.

7. Several factors make the task easier than it might seem. These factors also have a direct bearing on the orientation and direction of the movement. Most important is the fact that the responsibility for coordination and tactical direction is delegated to a small staff of key leaders. These people are dedicated activists and seem to know where they are going. Another – and related – factor is the interlocking structure of the peace groups. A number of the key activists are involved in more than one organization, and there is considerable interaction among the executives. The problem of lining up many diverse groups and coordinating action is thus simplified to some degree . . .

9. As the peace groups have coalesced over the past year and a half, ideological lines have become so blurred as to render conventional political classifications worthless. The various joint action groups are so conglomerate that it is difficult to stamp them with any one label without qualification. Control is the only valid indicator, and evidence of control by any one element is what is usually lacking. The peace movement, and even most of its constituent parts, is too big and too amorphous to be controlled by any one political faction.

10. In terms of the political spectrum and international connections, the activists generally range from somewhere left of center to the farthest limit of the Left. . . . The peace movement can be described in ideological terms only if one political element is dominant or exerts a controlling influence. A careful review of the evidence available on both domestic and foreign activity does not substantiate either conclusion in the case of any of the groups. . . .

   Marxist groups harbor deep hostilities toward each other; often in fact they seem more concerned about countering each other than about countering the nonCommunists.

12. As a result of their infiltration of the leadership of key peace groups, the Communists manage to exert disproportionate influence over the groups' policies and actions. It remains doubtful, however, that this influence is controlling . . .

Although plainly radical . . . SDS leaders are not interested in "prepackaged ideology" or excessive Communist guidance. These militants, who identify themselves as the New Left, generally look on Communists – especially those with foreign loyalties – as not only suspect but rather old hat . . .

On the basis of what we now know, we see no significant evidence that would prove Communist control or direction of the US peace movement or its leaders.

Source: Charles DeBenedetti, "A CIA Analysis of the Anti-Vietnam War Movement: October 1967," *Peace & Change*, vol. 9, no. 1 (Spring 1983), pp. 31–41.

Document 17

North Vietnamese Goals for the Tet Offensive

Local communist cadres received this 1 November 1967 directive explaining the goals and strategy for the Tet Offensive, the long-awaited general offensive and uprising.

This is to notify you that an offensive and uprising will take place in the very near future and we will mount stronger attacks on towns and cities, in coordination with the widespread movement in the rural areas. The enemy will be thrown into utmost confusion. No matter how violently the enemy may react, he cannot avoid collapse. This is not only a golden opportunity to liberate hamlets and villages but also an opportunity to liberate district seats, province capitals and South Viet-Nam as a whole.

Our victory is close at hand. The conditions are ripe. Our Party has carefully judged the situation. We must act and act fast. This is an opportunity to fulfill the aspirations of the entire people, of cadre, of each comrade and of our families . . .

How will the uprising be conducted?

There are two fundamental steps:

First, annihilate the enemy's political power. It is fundamental that we capture all tyrants from the village and hamlet administrative machinery and a number of spies. If we are not successful in this area the uprising will not be able to take place.

Second, organize our political power, specifically our district, village and hamlet administrative machinery.

To conduct an uprising, you must have a roster of all the tyrants and spies and be familiar with the way they live and where they live. Then use suicide cells to annihilate them by any means . . .

Conduct meetings and give information of the current situation (about 10 to 15 minutes). Make use of the populace immediately in sabotage and support activities and in raid operations against the spies. The masses should be encouraged to go on strike. Dig trenches and make spikes all night long, and contribute to the transformation of the terrain. All people in each family, regardless of their ages, should be encouraged to take part . . .

Source: "Directive from Province Party Standing Committee
to District and Local Party Organs on Forthcoming Offensive
and Uprisings, 1 November 1967," *Vietnam Documents
and Research Notes*, April 1968, reprinted in
Steven Cohen (ed.), *Vietnam* (New York: Alfred A.
Knopf, 1983), pp. 201–203.

Document 18

Report from Vietnam

Newscaster Walter Cronkite delivered this report on 27 February 1968 in the wake of the Tet Offensive.

We have been too often disappointed by the optimism of the American leaders, both in Vietnam and Washington, to have faith any longer in the silver linings they find in the darkest clouds. They may be right, that Hanoi's winter–spring offensive has been forced by the Communist realization that they could not win the longer war of attrition, and that the Communists hope that any success in the offensive will improve their position for eventual negotiations. It would improve their position, and it would also require our realization, that we should have had all along, that any negotiations must be that – negotiations, not the dictation of peace terms. For it seems now more certain than ever that the bloody experience of Vietnam is to end in a stalemate. This summer's almost certain standoff will either end in real give-and-take negotiations or terrible escalation; and for every means we have to escalate, the enemy can match us, and that applies to invasion of the North, the use of nuclear weapons, or the mere commitment of one hundred, or two hundred, or three hundred thousand more American troops to the battle. And with each escalation, the world comes closer to the brink of cosmic disaster.

To say that we are closer to victory today is to believe, in the face of the evidence, the optimists who have been wrong in the past. To suggest we are on the edge of defeat is to yield to unreasonable pessimism. To say that we are mired in stalemate seems the only realistic, yet unsatisfactory, conclusion. On the off chance that military and political analysts are right, in the next few months we must test the enemy's intentions, in case this is indeed his last big gasp before negotiations. But it is increasingly clear to this reporter that the only rational way out then will be to negotiate, not as victors, but as an honorable people who lived up to their pledge to defend democracy, and did the best they could.

Source: *Who, What, When, Where, Why: Report from Vietnam
by Walter Cronkite*. Originally broadcast 27 February,
1968 over the CBS Television Network, reprinted in
Peter Braestrup, *Big Story: How the American Press
and Television Reported the Crisis of Tet 1968 in
Vietnam and Washington*, 2 vols. (Boulder, CO:
Westview Press, 1977), II, pp. 188–189.

Document 19

"Peace in Vietnam and Southeast Asia"

During this 31 March 1968 televised address, President Lyndon Johnson announced a renewed effort for a negotiated settlement and withdrew from that year's presidential campaign.

Tonight, I renew the offer I made last August – to stop the bombardment of North Vietnam. We ask that talks begin promptly, that they be serious talks on the substance of peace. We assume that during those talks Hanoi will not take advantage of our restraint.

We are prepared to move immediately toward peace through negotiations . . .

Tonight, I have ordered our aircraft and our naval vessels to make no attacks on North Vietnam, except in the area north of the demilitarized zone where the continuing enemy buildup directly threatens allied forward positions and where the movements of their troops and supplies are clearly related to that threat . . .

Now, as in the past, the United States is ready to send its representatives to any forum, at any time, to discuss the means of bringing this ugly war to an end . . .

I call upon President Ho Chi Minh to respond positively, and favorably, to this new step toward peace . . .

Our presence there has always rested on this basic belief: The main burden of preserving their freedom must be carried out by them – by the South Vietnamese themselves.

We and our allies can only help to provide a shield behind which the people of South Vietnam can survive and can grow and develop. On their efforts – on their determination and resourcefulness – the outcome will ultimately depend . . .

We shall accelerate the reequipment of South Vietnam's armed forces – in order to meet the enemy's increased firepower. This will enable them progressively to undertake a larger share of combat operations against the Communist invaders . . .

I cannot promise that the initiative that I have announced tonight will be completely successful in achieving peace any more than the 30 others that we have undertaken and agreed to in recent years.

But it is our fervent hope that North Vietnam, after years of fighting that have left the issue unresolved, will now cease its efforts to achieve a military victory and will join with us in moving toward the peace table . . .

Our objective in South Vietnam has never been the annihilation of the enemy. It has been to bring about a recognition in Hanoi that its objective – taking over the South by force – could not be achieved.

We think that peace can be based on the Geneva Accords of 1954 – under political conditions that permit the South Vietnamese – all the South Vietnamese – to chart their course free of any outside domination or interference, from us or from someone else.

So tonight I reaffirm the pledge that we made at Manila – that we are prepared to withdraw our forces from South Vietnam as the other side withdraws its forces to the north, stops the infiltration, and the level of violence thus subsides . . .

Peace will come because Asians were willing to work for it – and to sacrifice for it – and to die by the thousands for it.

But let it never be forgotten: Peace will come also because America sent her sons to help secure it . . .

Yet, I believe that we must always be mindful of this one thing, whatever the trials and the tests ahead. The ultimate strength of our country and our cause will lie not in powerful weapons or infinite resources or boundless wealth, but will lie in the unity of our people . . .

There is division in the American house now. There is divisiveness among us all tonight. And holding the trust that is mine, as President of all the people, I cannot disregard the peril to the progress of the American people and the hope and the prospect of peace for all peoples . . .

Believing this as I do, I have concluded that I should not permit the Presidency to become involved in the partisan divisions that are developing in this political year.

With America's sons in the fields far away, with America's future under challenge right here at home, with our hopes and the world's hopes for peace in the balance every day, I do not believe that I should devote an hour or a day of my time to any personal partisan causes or to any duties other than the awesome duties of the office – the Presidency of your country.

Accordingly, I shall not seek, and I will not accept, the nomination of my party for another term as your President.

But let men everywhere know, however, that a strong, a confident, and a vigilant America stands ready tonight to seek an honorable peace – and stands ready tonight to defend an honored cause – whatever the price, whatever the burden, whatever the sacrifice that duty may require.

Source: *Weekly Compilation of Presidential Documents,*
vol. 4, no. 14 (8 April 1968), pp. 619–626.

Document 20

South Vietnam's Six Points for Peace

President Nguyen Van Thieu proposed these points to South Vietnam's National Assembly on 7 April 1969 as the basis for peace.

1. Communist aggression should stop . . .
2. Communist North Vietnamese and auxiliary troops and cadres should be completely withdrawn from the Republic of Viet-Nam . . .
3. The territories of the neighboring countries of the RVN should not be violated and used by Communist North Viet-Nam as bases and staging areas for aggression against the RVN . . .
4. The RVN adopts the policy of National Reconciliation.
   Those now fighting against us, who renounce violence, respect the laws, and faithfully abide by the democratic processes, will be welcomed as full members of the National Community . . .
5. The reunification of the two Viet-Nams is to be decided by the free choice of the entire population of Viet-Nam through democratic processes . . .
6. There must be an effective system of international control and reliable international guarantees against the resumption of Communist aggression . . .

Source: Robert J. McMahon (ed.), *Major Problems in the
History of the Vietnam War,* 3rd edn. (Boston,
MA: Houghton Mifflin, 2003), pp. 362–363.

Document 21

Silent Majority Speech

This speech, delivered by President Richard Nixon on 3 November 1969, appealed to the American public at a time of considerable antiwar activity.

In January I could only conclude that the precipitate withdrawal of American forces from Vietnam would be a disaster not only for South Vietnam but for the United States and for the cause of peace.

For the South Vietnamese, our precipitate withdrawal would inevitably allow the Communists to repeat the massacres which followed their takeover in the North 15 years before . . .

For the United States, this first defeat in our Nation's history would result in a collapse of confidence in American leadership, not only in Asia but throughout the world . . .

For these reasons, I rejected the recommendation that I should end the war by immediately withdrawing all of our forces. I chose instead to change American policy on both the negotiating front and battlefront . . .

It has become clear that the obstacle in negotiating an end to the war is not the President of the United States. It is not the South Vietnamese Government.

The obstacle is the other side's absolute refusal to show the least willingness to join us in seeking a just peace. And it will not do so while it is convinced that all it has to do is to wait for our next concession, and our next concession after that one, until it gets everything it wants.

There can now be no longer any question that progress in negotiation depends only on Hanoi's deciding to negotiate, to negotiate seriously . . .

At the time we launched our search for peace I recognized we might not succeed in bringing an end to the war through negotiation. I, therefore, put into effect another plan to bring peace – a plan which will bring the war to an end regardless of what happens on the negotiating front . . .

In the previous administration, we Americanized the war in Vietnam. In this administration, we are Vietnamizing the search for peace . . .

The Vietnamization plan was launched following Secretary Laird's visit to Vietnam in March. Under the plan, I ordered first a substantial increase in the training and equipment of South Vietnamese forces.

In July, on my visit to Vietnam, I changed General Abrams' orders so that they were consistent with the objectives of our new policies. Under the new orders, the primary mission of our troops is to enable the South Vietnamese forces to assume the full responsibility for the security of South Vietnam . . .

We have adopted a plan which we have worked out in cooperation with the South Vietnamese for the complete withdrawal of all US combat ground forces, and their replacement by South Vietnamese forces on an orderly scheduled timetable. This withdrawal will be made from strength and not from weakness. As South Vietnamese forces become stronger, the rate of American withdrawal can become greater . . .

For almost 200 years, the policy of this Nation has been made under our Constitution by those leaders in the Congress and the White House elected by all of the people. If a vocal minority, however fervent its cause, prevails over reason and the will of the majority, this Nation has no future as a free society . . .

Two hundred years ago this Nation was weak and poor. But even then, America was the hope of millions in the world. Today we have become the strongest and richest nation in the world. And the wheel of destiny has turned so that any hope the world has for the survival of peace and freedom will be determined by whether the American people have the moral stamina and the courage to meet the challenge of free world leadership.

Let historians not record that when America was the most powerful nation in the world we passed on the other side of the road and allowed the last hopes for peace and freedom of millions of people to be suffocated by the forces of totalitarianism.

And so tonight – to you, the great silent majority of my fellow Americans – I ask for your support.

I pledged in my campaign for the Presidency to end the war in a way that we could win the peace. I have initiated a plan of action which will enable me to keep that pledge.

The more support I can have from the American people, the sooner that pledge can be redeemed; for the more divided we are at home, the less likely the enemy is to negotiate at Paris.

Let us be united for peace. Let us also be united against defeat. Because let us understand: North Vietnam cannot defeat or humiliate the United States. Only Americans can do that . . .

Source: *Weekly Compilation of Presidential Documents*,
vol. 5, no. 45 (3 November 1969), pp. 1546–1555.

Document 22

The Invasion of Cambodia

Televised speech delivered by President Richard Nixon on 30 April 1970 to explain the US and South Vietnamese offensive into Cambodia

I have concluded that the actions of the enemy in the last 10 days clearly endanger the lives of Americans who are in Vietnam now and would constitute an unacceptable risk to those who will be there after withdrawal of another 150,000 . . .

For 5 years, neither the United States nor South Vietnam has moved against these enemy sanctuaries because we did not wish to violate the territory of a neutral nation. Even after the Vietnamese Communists began to expand these sanctuaries 4 weeks ago, we counseled patience to our South Vietnamese allies and imposed restraints on our own commanders . . .

In cooperation with the armed forces of South Vietnam, attacks are being launched this week to clean out major enemy sanctuaries on the Cambodian–Vietnam border . . .

Tonight, American and South Vietnamese units will attack the headquarters for the entire Communist military operation in South Vietnam.

This key control center has been occupied by the North Vietnamese and Vietcong for 5 years in blatant violation of Cambodian neutrality.

This is not an invasion of Cambodia. The areas in which these attacks will be launched are completely occupied and controlled by North Vietnamese forces. Our purpose is not to occupy the areas. Once enemy forces are driven out of these sanctuaries and once their military supplies are destroyed, we will withdraw . . .

My fellow Americans, we live in an age of anarchy, both abroad and at home. We see mindless attacks on all the great institutions which have been created by free civilizations in the last 500 years. Even here in the United States, great universities are being systematically destroyed . . .

If, when the chips are down, the world's most powerful nation, the United States of America, acts like a pitiful, helpless giant, the forces of totalitarianism and anarchy will threaten free nations and free institutions throughout the world.

It is not our power but our will and character that is being tested tonight . . .

Source: *Weekly Compilation of Presidential Documents*, vol. 6, no. 18 (4 May 1970), pp. 596–601.

Document 23

John Kerry Testimony

John Kerry of Vietnam Veterans Against the War testified before the US Senate Foreign Relations Committee on 22 April 1971.

I would like to talk on behalf of all those veterans and say that several months ago in Detroit we had an investigation at which over 150 honorably discharged, and many very highly decorated, veterans testified to war crimes committed in Southeast Asia. These were not isolated incidents but crimes committed on a day to day basis with the full awareness of officers at all levels of command . . .

They told stories that at times they had personally raped, cut off ears, cut off heads, taped wires from portable telephones to human genitals and turned up the power, cut off limbs, blown up bodies, randomly shot at civilians, razed villages in fashion reminiscent of Genghis Khan, shot cattle and dogs for fun, poisoned food stocks, and generally ravaged the countryside of South Vietnam in addition to the normal ravage of war and the normal and very particular ravaging which is done by the applied bombing power of this country.

We call this investigation the Winter Soldier Investigation. The term Winter Soldier is a play on words of Thomas Paine's in 1776 when he spoke of the Sunshine Patriots and summer time soldiers who deserted at Valley Forge because the going was rough . . .

Each day to facilitate the process by which the United States washes her hands of Vietnam someone has to give up his life so that the United States doesn't have to admit something that the entire world already knows, so that we can't say that we have made a mistake. Someone has to die so that President Nixon won't be, and these are his words, "the first President to lose a war."

We are asking Americans to think about that because how do you ask a man to be the last man to die in Vietnam? How do you ask a man to be the last man to die for a mistake? . . .

Finally, this administration has done us the ultimate dishonor. They have attempted to disown us and the sacrifices we made for this country. In their blindness and fear they have tried to deny that we are veterans or that we served in Nam. We do not need their testimony. Our own scars and stumps of limbs are witness enough for others and for ourselves.

We wish that a merciful God could wipe away our own memories of that service as easily as this administration has wiped away their memories of us. But all that they have done and all that they can do by this denial is to make more clear than ever our own determination to undertake one last mission – to search out and destroy the last vestige of this barbaric war, to pacify our own hearts, to conquer the hate and the fear that have driven this country these last ten years and more, so when 30 years from now our brothers go down the street without a leg, without an arm, or a face, and small boys ask why, we will be able to say "Vietnam" and not mean a desert, not a filthy obscene memory, but mean instead the place where America finally turned and where soldiers like us helped it in the turning.

Source: *Congressional Record*, 22nd Congress,
Session 1, pp. 13414–13416.

Document 24

South Vietnamese Analysis of the Easter Offensive

This summary of the 1972 Easter Offensive is from ARVN Lieutenant-General Ngo Quang Truong.

The importance and decisiveness of this effort were readily apparent by the forces Hanoi had committed – at least ten infantry divisions and hundreds of tanks and artillery pieces. The Hanoi leadership always timed its major efforts to exert maximum impact on American domestic politics. The 1972 Easter Offensive was in line with this policy. And true to their doctrinal precepts, the Communist leaders of North Vietnam evidenced little concern for personnel and equipment losses, provided that the ultimate objectives set forth by their Politbureau could be attained.

From its very beginning, this offensive was an ultimate challenge for South Vietnam. At various times in some geographical areas, victory appeared to be within reach of the enemy. Indeed, the initial stage of Hanoi's offensive had been successful beyond the capability of its forces to exploit . . . . The initial momentum of the NVA offensive was awesome . . .

Even though United States strength in South Vietnam had been greatly reduced, both logistic and combat support was responsive and effective. Immediately following the initial attacks by the enemy, the United States initiated an emergency program to provide support to battered RVNAF units on all battlefields to assist them in regaining their strength and initiative. Combat support was provided by massed air and naval firepower against NVA units, their supply lines and bases.

Injected with new vigor, ARVN units resisted with determination. The enemy's desperate attempt to overwhelm our units again with his local numerical superiority was countered with B-52 and tactical air strikes. As he increased his assaults with massed infantry, the heavier his losses became. Finally, this attrition caused his offensive to run out of steam . . .

In retrospect, Hanoi's conventional invasion of the South did not help it attain the major objectives desired. Although always the defender with an extremely disadvantageous strategic posture, South Vietnam emerged stronger than ever. Hanoi's effort had been thwarted by US–RVN determination. The American response during the enemy offensive was timely, forceful and decisive. This staunch resolve of the US to stand behind its ally stunned the enemy. Additionally, it brought about a strong feeling of self-assurance among the armed forces and population of South Vietnam . . .

Source: Ngo Quang Truong, "The Easter Offensive of 1972," *Indochina Series*, pp. 175–181, reprinted in Steven Cohen (ed.), *Vietnam* (New York: Alfred A. Knopf, 1983), pp. 325–327.

Document 25

Paris Peace Accords

This peace agreement was signed by the United States, North Vietnam, South Vietnam, and the Provisional Revolutionary Government on 27 January 1973.

Article 1

The United States and all other countries respect the independence, sovereignty, unity, and territorial integrity of Viet-Nam as recognized by the 1954 Geneva Agreements on Viet-Nam.

Article 2

A cease-fire shall be observed throughout South Viet-Nam as of 2400 hours G.M.T., on January 27, 1973.

At the same hour, the United States will stop all its military activities against the territory of the Democratic Republic of Viet-Nam by ground, air and naval forces, wherever they may be based, and end the mining of the territorial waters, ports, harbors, and waterways of the Democratic Republic of Viet-Nam. The United States will remove, permanently deactivate or destroy all the mines in the territorial waters, ports, harbors, and waterways of North Viet-Nam as soon as this Agreement goes into effect . . .

Article 3

(a) The United States forces and those of the other foreign countries allied with the United States and the Republic of Viet-Nam shall remain in-place pending the implementation of the plan of troop withdrawal . . .

(b) The armed forces of the two South Vietnamese parties shall remain in-place. The Two-Party Joint Military Commission described in Article 17 shall determine the areas controlled by each party and the modalities of stationing . . .

Article 4

The United States will not continue its military involvement or intervene in the internal affairs of South Viet-Nam.

Article 5

Within sixty days of the signing of this Agreement, there will be a total withdrawal from South Viet-Nam of troops, military advisers, and military personnel, including technical military personnel and military personnel associated with the pacification program, armaments, munitions, and war material of the United States and those of the other foreign countries mentioned in Article 3 (a). Advisers from the above-mentioned countries to all paramilitary organizations and the police force will also be withdrawn within the same period of time.

Article 6

The dismantlement of all military bases in South Viet-Nam of the United States and of the other foreign countries mentioned in Article 3 (a) shall be completed within sixty days of the signing of this Agreement.

Article 7

From the enforcement of the cease-fire to the formation of the government provided for in Article 9 (b) and 14 of this Agreement, the two South Vietnamese parties shall not accept the introduction of troops, military advisers, and military personnel including technical military personnel, armaments, munitions, and war material into South Viet-Nam. . . .

Article 8

(a) The return of captured military personnel and foreign civilians of the parties shall be carried out simultaneously with and completed not later than the same day as the troop withdrawal mentioned in Article 5. The parties shall exchange complete lists of the above-mentioned captured military personnel and foreign civilians on the day of the signing of this Agreement . . .

Article 9

(b) The South Vietnamese people shall decide themselves the political future of South Viet-Nam through genuinely free and democratic general elections under international supervision . . .

Article 10

The two South Vietnamese parties undertake to respect the cease-fire and maintain peace in South Viet-Nam, settle all matters of contention through negotiations, and avoid all armed conflict . . .

Article 15

The reunification of Viet-Nam shall be carried out step by step through peaceful means on the basis of discussions and agreements between North and South Viet-Nam, without coercion or annexation by either party, and without foreign interference. The time for reunification will be agreed upon by North and South Viet-Nam.

Pending reunification:

(a) The military demarcation line between the two zones at the 17th parallel is only provisional and not a political or territorial boundary, as provided for in paragraph 6 of the Final Declaration of the 1954 Geneva Conference . . .
(d) North and South Viet-Nam shall not join any military alliance or military bloc and shall not allow foreign powers to maintain military bases, troops, military advisers, and military personnel on their respective territories, as stipulated in the 1954 Geneva Agreements on Viet-Nam . . .

Article 21

In pursuance of its traditional policy, the United States will contribute to healing the wounds of war and to postwar reconstruction of the Democratic Republic of Viet-Nam and throughout Indochina. . . .

Source: *United States Treaties and Other International Agreements,* vol. 24, part 1, 1973, pp. 1–224.

Document 26

President Nixon Promises Postwar Reconstruction

This 1 February 1973 letter from President Richard Nixon to Pham Van Dong, kept secret until its declassification in May 1977, promised as much as $4.75 billion in reconstruction aid to North Vietnam.

The President wishes to inform the Democratic Republic of Vietnam of the principles which will govern United States participation in the postwar reconstruction of North Vietnam. As indicated in Article 21 of the Agreement on Ending the War and Restoring Peace in Vietnam signed in Paris on Jan. 27, 1973, the United States undertakes this participation in accordance with its traditional policies. These principles are as follows:

1. The Government of the United States of America will contribute to postwar reconstruction in North Vietnam without any political conditions.
2. Preliminary United States studies indicate that the appropriate programs for the United States contribution to postwar reconstruction will fall in the range of $3.25 billion of grant aid over five years. Other forms of aid will be agreed upon between the two parties. This estimate is subject to revision and to detailed discussion between the Government of the United States and the Government of the Democratic Republic [of] Vietnam.
3. The United States will propose to the Democratic Republic of Vietnam the establishment of a United States–North Vietnamese Joint Economic Commission within 30 days from the date of this message.
4. The function of the commission will be to develop programs for the United States contribution to reconstruction of North Vietnam. This United States contribution will be based upon such factors as:

    (a) the needs of North Vietnam arising from the dislocation of war;
    (b) the requirements for postwar reconstruction in the agricultural and industrial sectors of North Vietnam's economy.

5. The Joint Economic Commission will have an equal number of representatives from each side. It will agree upon a mechanism to administer the program which will constitute the United States

contribution to the reconstruction of North Vietnam. The commission will attempt to complete this agreement within 60 days after its establishment.

6. The two members of the commission will function on the principle of respect for each other's sovereignty, noninterference in each other's internal affairs, equality and mutual benefit. The offices of the commission will be located at a place to be agreed upon by the United States and the Democratic Republic of Vietnam.

7. The United States considers that the implementation of the foregoing principles will prompt economic, trade and other relations between the United States of America and the Democratic Republic of Vietnam and will contribute to insuring a stable and lasting peace in Indochina. These principles accord with the spirit of Chapter VIII of the Agreement on Ending the War and Restoring Peace in Vietnam which was signed in Paris on Jan. 27, 1973.

. . . It is understood that the recommendations of the Joint Economic Commission mentioned in the President's note to the Prime Minister will be implemented by each member in accordance with its own constitutional provisions.

. . . In regard to other forms of aid, United States studies indicate that the appropriate programs could fall in the range of $1 billion to $1.5 billion, depending on food and other commodity needs of the Democratic Republic of Vietnam.

Source: *New York Times*, 20 May 1977, p. A17.

Document 27

Resignation Speech of Nguyen Van Thieu

Delivered by South Vietnamese President Nguyen Van Thieu on 21 April 1975

At the time, there was collusion between the communists and the United States with a view to reaching the agreement of 26th October 1972. This agreement, which I spent much time explaining to our compatriots . . . was an agreement by which the United States sold South Vietnam to the communists. I had enough courage to tell Secretary of State Kissinger at that time the following: if you accept this agreement, this means you accept to sell South Vietnam to the North Vietnamese communists. As for me, if I accept this agreement, I will be a traitor and seller of the South Vietnamese people and territory to the communists. If you accept it, this is for US interests or for some private reason which I do not know about. It is a sharing of interests among you powers that I do not know about. You make some concessions or exchanges among you. You want to sell the interests and lives of the South Vietnamese. As for me, a Vietnamese, I cannot do so.

I refused to accept this agreement. I opposed this agreement for three months . . .

I have therefore told them (the Americans): you have asked us to do something that you failed to do with half a million powerful troops and skilled commanders and with nearly 300 billion dollars in expenditures over six long years. If I do not say that you were defeated by the communists in Vietnam, I must modestly say that you did not win either. But you found an honourable way out. And at present, when our army lacks weapons, ammunition, helicopters, aircraft and B-52s, you ask us to do an impossible thing like filling up the ocean with stones . . .

A ruler of a country can enjoy either honour or disgrace. He must accept this so he can lead the people. If I have some good points, the compatriots will praise me even if I do not want it. But if I have some bad points and errors, I am ready to accept judgements and accusations from the compatriots. Today, as I leave my office, I ask the compatriots, combatants and cadres, together with all popular organizations and religions, to forgive those errors I have committed against the nation during my presidential term.

I am resigning but not deserting. From this moment, I place myself at the service of the President, the people and the army. As I step down, Mr. Tran Van Huong will become President and our nation will not lose anything. Perhaps our country will gain another combatant on the battlefront. I will stand shoulder to shoulder with the compatriots and combatants to defend the country . . .

Source: Steven Cohen (ed.), Vietnam (New York:
Alfred A. Knopf, 1983), pp. 413–415.

Document 28

Le Duan's Victory Speech

Le Duan delivered this speech at a 15 May 1975 victory celebration in Hanoi.

Today, with boundless joy, throughout the country our 45 million people are jubilantly celebrating the great victory we have won in the general offensive and uprising this Spring of 1975, in completely defeating the war of aggression and the neocolonialist rule of US imperialism, liberating the whole of the southern half of our country so dear to our hearts and gloriously ending the longest, most difficult and greatest patriotic war ever waged in the history of our people's struggle against foreign aggression . . .

We hail the new era in our nation's 4,000-year history – era of brilliant prospects for the development of a peaceful, independent, reunified, democratic, prosperous and strong Viet Nam, an era in which the labouring people have become the complete masters of their destiny and will pool their physical and mental efforts to build a plentiful and happy life for themselves and for thousands of generations to come.

This glory belongs to our great President Ho Chi Minh, the outstanding national hero who brought fame to our land, the first Vietnamese Communist who founded and trained our Party, who steered the ship of the Vietnamese revolution through many a storm to enable it to reach the shore of glory today. In this stirring atmosphere of total victory, our hearts are filled with great emotion at the memory of our beloved Uncle Ho . . .

Source: Le Duan, *Le Duan: Selected Writings*, pp. 516–540,
reprinted in Spencer C. Tucker (ed.), *Encyclopedia of the
Vietnam War* (Santa Barbara, CA: ABC–CLIO,
1998), pp. 1082–1085.

Further Reading

The place of publication is New York unless otherwise stated.

Primary Sources and General Works

The volumes on Vietnam in the US State Department series, *Foreign Relations of the United States* (Washington, DC: Government Printing Office), offer perhaps the most valuable source of documents. *The Public Papers of the Presidents of the United States* (Washington, DC: Government Printing Office), is another useful collection. Several valuable edited document collections exist. These include David Barrett (ed.), *Lyndon Johnson's Vietnam Papers: A Documentary Collection* (College Station: Texas A&M University Press, 1997); Marvin Gettleman, Jane Franklin, Marilyn Young, and H. Bruce Franklin (eds.), *Vietnam and America: A Documented History*, 2nd edn. (Grove Press, 1995); William Appleman Williams, Thomas McCormick, Lloyd Gardner, and Walter LaFeber (eds.), *America in Vietnam: A Documentary History* (Norton, 1985); and Gareth Porter (ed.), *Vietnam: The Definitive Documentation of Human Decisions*, 2 vols. (Stanfordville, NY: Coleman, 1979). Still useful are the *Pentagon Papers*, published in various forms. Neil Sheehan, et al., *The Pentagon Papers as published by the New York Times* (Bantam Books, 1971) is the best introduction, but a larger collection is *The Pentagon Papers: The Defense Department History of United States Decisionmaking on Vietnam*, Senator Gravel edition, 5 vols. (Boston: Beacon Press, 1971–1972). For sections involving peace initiatives, see George C. Herring (ed.), *The Secret Diplomacy of the Vietnam War: The Negotiating Volumes of the Pentagon Papers* (Austin: University of Texas Press, 1983).

More extensive collections are available on microfilm. A select sample would include *The John F. Kennedy National Security Files: Vietnam: National Security Files, 1961–1963* (Frederick, MD: University Publications of America); *The Lyndon B. Johnson National Security*

Files: Vietnam: National Security Files, November 1963–June 1965 (Frederick, MD: University Publications of America, 1992); *Records of the Military Assistance Command Vietnam* (Frederick, MD: University Publications of America, 1988); *U.S. Armed Forces in Vietnam, 1954–1975* (Frederick, MD: University Publications of America, 1983); *The Peers Inquiry of the Massacre at My Lai* (Bethesda, MD: University Publications of America, 1996); *Vietnam, the Media, and Public Support for the War* (Frederick, MD: University Publications of America); and *Transcripts and Files of the Paris Peace Talks on Vietnam, 1968–1973* (Frederick, MD: University Publications of America).

There are several good surveys of the war. Among the best accounts by historians are George C. Herring, *America's Longest War: The United States and Vietnam, 1950–1975*, 5th edn. (McGraw-Hill, 2014); Mark Philip Bradley, *Vietnam at War* (Oxford University Press, 2009); Gary R. Hess, *Vietnam and the United States: Origins and Legacy of War* (Boston: Twayne, 1990); Mark Atwood Lawrence, *The Vietnam War: A Concise International History* (Oxford University Press, 2008); George Donnelson Moss, *Vietnam: An American Ordeal*, 6th edn. (Boston: Prentice Hall, 2010); John Prados, *Vietnam: The History of an Unwinnable War, 1945–1975* (Lawrence: University Press of Kansas, 2009); Robert D. Schulzinger, *A Time For War: The United States and Vietnam, 1941–1975* (Oxford University Press, 1997); William S. Turley, *The Second Indochina War: A Concise Political and Military History*, 2nd edn. (Lanham, MD: Rowman & Littlefield, 2009); and Marilyn B. Young, *The Vietnam Wars, 1945–1990* (HarperCollins, 1991). These works represent the dominant scholarly view of the war, known as the orthodox interpretation, which argues that, for various reasons and to varying degrees, the war was a misguided policy. Similar views from journalists include A. J. Langguth, *Our Vietnam: The War 1954–1975* (Simon & Schuster, 2000); and Stanley Karnow, *Vietnam: A History* (Viking, 1983). An outstanding multivolume history of the war is William C. Gibbons, *The U.S. Government and the Vietnam War: Executive and Legislative Roles and Relationships*, 4 vols. (Princeton, NJ: Princeton University Press, 1985–1995).

Among revisionist accounts, Guenter Lewy, *America in Vietnam* (Oxford University Press, 1978), defends the US from war crimes charges and argues that a different military strategy would have won the war. Michael Lind, *Vietnam, The Necessary War: A Reinterpretation of America's Most Disastrous Military Conflict* (Free Press, 1999), defends the war but does not believe it could have been won.

The best reference work on the war is Spencer C. Tucker (ed.), *Encyclopedia of the Vietnam War: A Political, Social, and Military History*, 3 vols. (Santa Barbara, CA: ABC–CLIO, 1998). Useful essay collections include Marc Jason Gilbert (ed.), *Why the North Won the Vietnam War*

(Palgrave, 2002); and Mitchell K. Hall (ed.), *Vietnam War Era: People and Perspectives* (Santa Barbara, CA: ABC–CLIO, 2009).

Chapter 1

For an introduction to Vietnamese history, consult Joseph Buttinger, *A Dragon Defiant: A Short History of Vietnam* (Praeger, 1972). An excellent background of Vietnam's revolution is David G. Marr, *Vietnam 1945: The Quest for Power* (Berkeley: University of California Press, 1995). For works dealing with the French–Indochina War, the place to start is Fredrik Logevall's Pulitzer Prize-winning *Embers of War: The Fall of an Empire and the Making of America's Vietnam* (Random House, 2012). Bernard Fall, *Hell in a Very Small Place: The Siege of Dien Bien Phu* (Philadelphia: J.B. Lippincott, 1967); and Martin Windrow, *The Last Valley: Dien Bien Phu and the French Defeat in Vietnam* (Cambridge, MA: Da Capo, 2004), cover the climactic battle. The implications for America are covered in Melanie Billings-Yun, *Decision Against War: Eisenhower and Dien Bien Phu, 1954* (Columbia University Press, 1988). For the Geneva Conference see Robert Randle, *Geneva 1954: The Settlement of the Indochinese War* (Princeton, NJ: Princeton University Press, 1969); and James Cable, *The Geneva Conference of 1954 on Indochina* (St. Martin's Press, 1986).

Several books detail the development of Vietnamese nationalism, including William J. Duiker, *Sacred War: Nationalism and Revolution in a Divided Vietnam* (McGraw-Hill, 1995); and William J. Duiker, *The Communist Road to Power in Vietnam* (Boulder, CO: Westview Press, 1981). For North Vietnam's approach to war, see Pierre Asselin, *Hanoi's Road to the Vietnam War, 1954–1965* (Berkeley: University of California Press, 2013); and Lien-Hang T. Nguyen, *Hanoi's War: An International History of the War for Peace in Vietnam* (Chapel Hill: University of North Carolina Press, 2012). The most complete history in English of Ho Chi Minh is William J. Duiker, *Ho Chi Minh: A Life* (Hyperion, 2000). For Vo Nguyen Giap, see Peter Macdonald, *Giap: The Victor in Vietnam* (Norton, 1993). David W.P. Elliott, *The Vietnamese War: Revolution and Social Change in the Mekong Delta, 1930–1975* (Armonk, NY: M.E. Sharpe, 2003); David Hunt, *Vietnam's Southern Revolution: From Peasant Insurrection to Total War* (Amherst: University of Massachusetts Press, 2008); Eric M. Bergerud, *The Dynamics of Defeat: The Vietnam War in Hau Nghia Province* (Boulder, CO: Westview Press, 1991); and Jeffrey Race, *War Comes to Long An: Revolutionary Conflict in a Vietnamese Province* (Berkeley: University of California Press, 1972), analyze revolution at the local level.

Among works revealing the Vietnamese perspective during the American phase of the war, Michael Lee Lanning and Dan Cragg, *Inside the*

NVA: The Real Story of North Vietnam's Armed Forces (Fawcett Columbine, 1992); and Douglas Pike, *PAVN: Peoples Army of Vietnam* (San Rafael, CA: Presidio Press, 1986), address the North Vietnamese military. Robert K. Brigham, *Guerrilla Diplomacy: The NLF's Foreign Relations and the Viet Nam War* (Ithaca, NY: Cornell University Press, 1998); and Douglas Pike, *Viet Cong: National Liberation Front of South Vietnam*, revised (Cambridge, MA: MIT Press, 1972), examine the National Liberation Front. Other valuable books include John Prados, *The Blood Road: The Ho Chi Minh Trail and the Vietnam War* (Wiley, 1999); Tom Mangold and John Penycate, *The Tunnels of Cu Chi* (Random House, 1985); James Trullinger, *Village at War: An Account of Revolution in Vietnam* (Longman, 1980); and Jon M. Van Dyke, *North Vietnam's Strategy for Survival* (Palo Alto, CA: Pacific Books, 1972).

The roots of American involvement are found in Ronald H. Spector, *Advice and Support: The Early Years of the U.S. Army in Vietnam, 1941–1960* (Free Press, 1985); George McT. Kahin, *Intervention: How America Became Involved in Vietnam* (Knopf, 1986); Andrew J. Rotter, *The Path to Vietnam: Origins of the American Commitment to Southeast Asia* (Ithaca, NY: Cornell University Press, 1987); Mark Atwood Lawrence, *Assuming the Burden: Europe and the American Commitment to War in Vietnam* (Berkeley: University of California Press, 2005); and Kathryn C. Statler, *Replacing France: The Origins of American Intervention in Vietnam* (Lexington: University Press of Kentucky, 2007). Mark Bradley, *Imagining Vietnam and America: The Making of Postcolonial Vietnam, 1919–1950* (Chapel Hill: University of North Carolina Press, 2000), includes more of the Vietnamese perspective.

For the US commitment during the Eisenhower years, see Robert Scigliano, *South Vietnam: Nation Under Stress* (Boston: Houghton Mifflin, 1963); David L. Anderson, *Trapped By Success: The Eisenhower Administration and Vietnam, 1953–1961* (Columbia University Press, 1991); Joseph G. Morgan, *The Vietnam Lobby: The American Friends of Vietnam, 1955–1975* (Chapel Hill: University of North Carolina Press, 1997); and John Ernst, *Forging a Fateful Alliance: Michigan State University and the Vietnam War* (East Lansing: Michigan State University Press, 1998). The rise of Ngo Dinh Diem is covered in Edward Miller, *Misalliance: Ngo Dinh Diem, the United States, and the Fate of South Vietnam* (Cambridge, MA: Harvard University Press, 2013); Seth Jacobs, *Cold War Mandarin: Ngo Dinh Diem and the Origins of America's War in Vietnam, 1950–1963* (Lanham, MD: Rowman & Littlefield, 2006); and Seth Jacobs, *America's Miracle Man in Vietnam: Ngo Dinh Diem, Religion, Race, and U.S. Intervention in Southeast Asia* (Durham, NC: Duke University Press, 2004).

Debate over President Kennedy's intentions is found in John M. Newman, *JFK and Vietnam: Deception, Intrigue, and the Struggle for Power* (Warner Books, 1992); David E. Kaiser, *American Tragedy: Kennedy,*

Johnson, and the Origins of the Vietnam War (Cambridge, MA: Belknap Press, 2000); and Howard Jones, *Death of a Generation: How the Assassinations of Diem and JFK Prolonged the Vietnam War* (Oxford University Press, 2003). David Halberstam, *The Best and the Brightest* (Random House, 1972), highlights the attitudes of early US decision makers. The most notable revisionist account of the early years is Mark Moyar, *Triumph Forsaken: The Vietnam War, 1954–1965* (Cambridge, UK: Cambridge University Press, 2006), which defends South Vietnam as a US vital interest, condemns the Diem coup as America's greatest error, and castigates Lyndon Johnson's lack of aggression for squandering previous gains.

Events in the Gulf of Tonkin are recounted in Edwin E. Moise, *Tonkin Gulf and the Escalation of the Vietnam War* (Chapel Hill: University of North Carolina Press, 1996); and Joseph C. Goulden, *Truth is the First Casualty: The Gulf of Tonkin Affair – Illusion and Reality* (Chicago: Rand McNally, 1969).

Chapter 2

First-hand accounts of the Johnson administration begin with Lyndon Baines Johnson, *The Vantage Point: Perspectives of the Presidency, 1963–1969* (Holt, Rinehart and Winston, 1971). For insights into Johnson's thinking, see Michael Beschloss (ed.), *Taking Charge: The Johnson White House Tapes, 1963–1964* (Simon & Schuster, 1997). Other memoirs from his administration include Robert McNamara with Brian VanDeMark, *In Retrospect: The Tragedy and Lessons of Vietnam* (Times Books, 1995); Dean Rusk with Richard Rusk, *As I Saw It* (Norton, 1990); George Ball, *The Past Has Another Pattern* (Norton, 1982); and Clark Clifford, *Counsel to the President* (Random House, 1991).

President Johnson's decisions regarding the war are found in Larry Berman, *Lyndon Johnson's War: The Road to Stalemate in Vietnam* (Norton, 1989); George C. Herring, *LBJ and Vietnam: A Different Kind of War* (Austin: University of Texas Press, 1994); Lloyd C. Gardner, *Pay Any Price: Lyndon Johnson and the Wars for Vietnam* (Chicago: Ivan Dee, 1995); Michael H. Hunt, *Lyndon Johnson's War: America's Cold War Crusade in Vietnam, 1945–1968* (Hill and Wang, 1996); and Fredrik Logevall, *Choosing War: The Lost Chance for Peace and the Escalation of War in Vietnam* (Berkeley: University of California Press, 1999). Other works on Johnson include Brian VanDeMark, *Into the Quagmire: Lyndon Johnson and the Escalation of the Vietnam War* (Oxford University Press, 1991); and David M. Barrett, *Uncertain Warriors: Lyndon Johnson and His Vietnam Advisers* (Lawrence: University Press of Kansas, 1993). For scholarly evaluations of other government leaders, see William C. Berman, *William Fulbright and the Vietnam War*

(Kent, OH: Kent State University Press, 1988); David DiLeo, *George Ball, Vietnam, and the Rethinking of Containment* (Chapel Hill: University of North Carolina Press, 1991); and Deborah Shapley, *Promise and Power: The Life and Times of Robert McNamara* (Boston: Little, Brown, 1993). For the war's impact on politics, see Walter LaFeber, *The Deadly Bet: LBJ, Vietnam, and the 1968 Election* (Lanham, MD: Rowman & Littlefield, 2005).

For coverage of the air war, Mark Clodfelter, *The Limits of Air Power: The American Bombing of North Vietnam* (Free Press, 1989); Earl H. Tilford Jr., *Crosswinds: The Air Force's Setup in Vietnam* (College Station: Texas A&M University Press, 1993); and Ronald B. Frankum Jr., *Like Rolling Thunder: The Air War in Vietnam, 1964–1975* (Lanham, MD: Rowman & Littlefield, 2005) provide good surveys. William Buckingham Jr., *Operation Ranch Hand: The Air Force and Herbicides in Southeast Asia, 1961–1971* (Washington, DC: Office of Air Force History, 1982), focuses on defoliation.

The early years of America's ground war appear in Neil Sheehan, *A Bright Shining Lie: John Paul Vann and America in Vietnam* (Vintage, 1988), a superb look at the war built around one of its most significant personalities; Harold G. Moore and Joseph L. Galloway, *We Were Soldiers Once . . . and Young* (HarperPerennial, 1993), which covers the 1965 battles in the Ia Drang Valley; Gregory Daddis, *No Sure Victory: Measuring U.S. Army Effectiveness and Progress in the Vietnam War* (Oxford University Press, 2011); John M. Carland, *Combat Operations: Stemming the Tide, May 1965 to October 1966* (Washington, DC: Center of Military History, 2000); and George L. MacGarrigle, *Combat Operations: Taking the Offensive, October 1966 to October 1967* (Washington, DC: Center of Military History, 1998). See also Gregory Daddis, *Westmoreland's War: Reassessing American Strategy in Vietnam* (Oxford University Press, 2014), provides a revised assessment of an often derided military leader. The 1968 defense of Khe Sanh is covered in Robert Pisor, *The End of the Line: The Siege of Khe Sanh* (Norton, 1982); and John Prados and Ray Stubbe, *Valley of Decision: The Siege of Khe Sanh* (Boston: Houghton Mifflin, 1991). Robert Buzzanco, *Masters of War: Military Dissent and Politics in the Vietnam Era* (Cambridge, UK: Cambridge University Press, 1996), explores military–civilian relations. Kyle Longley, *Grunts: The American Combat Soldier in Vietnam* (Armonk, NY: M.E. Sharpe, 2008), analyzes the experiences of US combat soldiers, while Robert K. Brigham, *ARVN: Life and Death in the South Vietnamese Army* (Lawrence: University Press of Kansas, 2006), does the same for Saigon's forces.

Vietnam's relationship with its major allies is the subject of Ilya Gaiduk, *The Soviet Union and the Vietnam War* (Chicago: Ivan Dee, 1996); Qiang Zhai, *China and the Vietnam Wars, 1950–1975* (Chapel Hill: University of North Carolina Press, 2000); and Douglas Pike,

Vietnam and the Soviet Union: Anatomy of an Alliance (Boulder, CO: Westview Press, 1987).

Chapter 3

The Vietnam era antiwar movement has attracted a great deal of attention from scholars. Surveys include Charles DeBenedetti with Charles Chatfield, *An American Ordeal: The Antiwar Movement of the Vietnam Era* (Syracuse, NY: Syracuse University Press, 1990); Nancy Zaroulis and Gerald Sullivan, *Who Spoke Up? American Protest Against the War in Vietnam, 1963–1975* (Garden City, NY: Doubleday, 1984); Melvin Small, *Antiwarriors: The Vietnam War and the Battle For America's Hearts and Minds* (Wilmington, DE: Scholarly Resources, 2002); and Tom Wells, *The War Within: America's Battle over Vietnam* (Berkeley: University of California Press, 1994). For a retrospective look, see Simon Hall, *Rethinking the American Anti-War Movement* (Routledge, 2012). Specific antiwar constituencies are covered in Mitchell K. Hall, *Because of Their Faith: CALCAV and Religious Opposition to the Vietnam War* (Columbia University Press, 1990); Andrew E. Hunt, *The Turning: A History of Vietnam Veterans Against the War* (New York University Press, 1999); and Kenneth J. Heineman, *Campus Wars: The Peace Movement at American State Universities in the Vietnam Era* (New York University Press, 1993). For strategies, consult Michael S. Foley, *Confronting the War Machine: Draft Resistance During the Vietnam War* (Chapel Hill: University of North Carolina Press, 2003); and Louis Menashe and Ronald Radosh (eds.), *Teach-ins USA: Reports, Opinions and Documents* (Praeger, 1967). Personal accounts include Fred Halstead, *Out Now: A Participant's Account of the American Movement against the Vietnam War* (Monad Press, 1978); and Norman Mailer, *The Armies of the Night* (New American Library, 1968). Melvin Small, *Johnson, Nixon and the Doves* (New Brunswick, NJ: Rutgers University Press, 1988), is a groundbreaking study of the movement's political impact. Lawrence Baskir and William Strauss, *Chance and Circumstance: The Draft, the War and the Vietnam Generation* (Vintage, 1978), looks at how the war affected the baby boomer generation.

A good introduction to organized support for the war is Sandra Scanlon, *The Pro-War Movement: Domestic Support for the Vietnam War and the Making of Modern American Conservatism* (Amherst: University of Massachusetts Press, 2013). Andrew L. Johns, *Vietnam's Second Front: Domestic Politics, the Republican Party, and the War* (Lexington: University Press of Kentucky, 2010); and Joseph A. Fry, *Debating Vietnam: Fulbright, Stennis, and Their Senate Hearings* (Lanham, MD: Rowman & Littlefield, 2006), examine congressional involvement in the war.

The Tet Offensive was perhaps the war's most crucial event. Among the best examinations are David F. Schmitz, *The Tet Offensive: Politics,*

War, and Public Opinion (Lanham, MD: Rowman & Littlefield, 2005); James H. Willbanks, *The Tet Offensive: A Concise History* (Columbia University Press, 2007); Marc Jason Gilbert and William Head (eds.), *The Tet Offensive* (Westport, CT: Praeger, 1996); James J. Wirtz, *The Tet Offensive: Intelligence Failure in War* (Ithaca, NY: Cornell University Press, 1991); and Don Oberdorfer, *Tet* (Garden City, NY: Doubleday, 1971). For an account that carries the story further, see Ronald H. Spector, *After Tet: The Bloodiest Year in Vietnam* (Free Press, 1993).

Media coverage of the war has been the subject of much controversy. Robert Elegant, "How to Lose a War," *Encounter*, 57 (1981), pp. 73–90, and Peter Braestrup, *Big Story: How the American Press and Television Reported and Interpreted the Crisis of Tet 1968 in Vietnam and Washington* (Boulder, CO: Westview Press, 1977), are both critical of press coverage. Refuting their conclusions are Daniel C. Hallin, *The "Uncensored War": The Media and Vietnam* (Oxford University Press, 1986); William M. Hammond, *Reporting Vietnam: Media and Military at War* (Lawrence: University Press of Kansas, 1998); and Clarence R. Wyatt, *Paper Soldiers: The American Press and the Vietnam War* (Norton, 1993). Melvin Small, *Covering Dissent: The Media and the Anti-Vietnam War Movement* (New Brunswick, NJ: Rutgers University Press, 1994), analyzes press coverage of the antiwar movement.

Chapter 4

Memoirs from the Nixon White House include Richard Nixon, *RN: The Memoirs of Richard Nixon* (Grossett & Dunlap, 1978); Henry Kissinger, *Ending the Vietnam War: A History of America's Involvement in and Extrication From the Vietnam War* (Simon & Schuster, 2003); and H.R. Haldeman, *The Haldeman Diaries* (Putnam, 1994). Scholarly works on Richard Nixon include Melvin Small, *The Presidency of Richard Nixon* (Lawrence: University Press of Kansas, 1999); and Stephen Ambrose, *Nixon*, 3 vols. (Simon & Schuster, 1987–1991). For a Vietnam focus, see Jeffrey Kimball, *Nixon's Vietnam War* (Lawrence: University Press of Kansas, 1998); David F. Schmitz, *Richard Nixon and the Vietnam War: The End of the American Century* (Lanham, MD: Rowman & Littlefield, 2014); and Larry Berman, *No Peace, No Honor: Nixon, Kissinger, and Betrayal in Vietnam* (Free Press, 2001). For Henry Kissinger, see Walter Isaacson, *Kissinger: A Biography* (Simon & Schuster, 1992); and William Shawcross, *Sideshow: Kissinger, Nixon and the Destruction of Cambodia* (Pocket Books, 1979).

For military affairs during the Nixon years, see Jeffrey J. Clarke, *Advice and Support: The Final Years, 1965–1973* (Washington, DC: Center of Military History, 1988); Dale Andradé, *America's Last Vietnam Battle: Halting Hanoi's 1972 Easter Offensive* (Lawrence: University Press of Kansas, 2001); and Lewis Sorley, *A Better War: The Unexamined*

Victories and Final Tragedy of America's Last Years in Vietnam (San Diego: Harvest/Harcourt, 1999). "Cincinnatus", *Self-Destruction: The Disintegration and Decay of the United States Army during the Vietnam Era* (Norton, 1981); and Shelby L. Stanton, *The Rise and Fall of an American Army: U.S. Ground Forces in Vietnam, 1965–1973* (Dell, 1985), detail problems within the armed forces.

Among those who address Vietnam's "other war" of pacification are Kevin M. Boylan, *Losing Binh Dinh: The Failure of Pacification and Vietnamization, 1969–1971* (Lawrence: University Press of Kansas, 2016); Thomas L. Ahern Jr., *Vietnam Declassified: The CIA and Counterinsurgency* (Lexington: University Press of Kentucky, 2010); and Douglas Blaufarb, *The Counterinsurgency Era: U.S. Doctrine and Performance* (Free Press, 1977). For the Phoenix program, Dale Andradé, *Ashes to Ashes: The Phoenix Program and the Vietnam War* (Lexington, MA: Lexington Books, 1990); and Douglas Valentine, *The Phoenix Program* (William Morrow, 1990), are critical, while Mark Moyar, *Phoenix and the Birds of Prey: The CIA's Secret Campaign to Destroy the Viet Cong* (Annapolis, MD: Naval Institute Press, 1997), challenges that interpretation.

The story of the My Lai Massacre appears in William Thomas Allison, *My Lai: An American Atrocity in the Vietnam War* (Baltimore: Johns Hopkins University Press, 2012); Michael Bilton and Kevin Sim, *Four Hours in My Lai* (Viking, 1992); Seymour M. Hersh, *My Lai 4: A Report on the Massacre and its Aftermath* (Random House, 1970); Michal R. Belknap, *The Vietnam War on Trial: The My Lai Massacre and the Court-Martial of Lieutenant Calley* (Lawrence: University Press of Kansas, 2002); and David L. Anderson (ed.), *Facing My Lai: Moving Beyond the Massacre* (Lawrence: University Press of Kansas, 1998). Nick Turse, *Kill Anything That Moves: The Real American War in Vietnam* (Metropolitan Books, 2013), argues that My Lai was unusual only in degree.

For secondary accounts of the Pentagon Papers, see David Rudenstine, *The Day the Presses Stopped: A History of the Pentagon Papers Case* (Berkeley: University of California Press, 1996); and Sanford Ungar, *The Papers and the Papers* (Dutton, 1972).

Oral histories and personal accounts document much of the American experience. Among the best are Christian G. Appy, *Patriots: The Vietnam War Remembered From All Sides* (Penguin, 2003); Christian G. Appy, *Working-Class War: American Combat Soldiers and Vietnam* (Chapel Hill: University of North Carolina Press, 1993); Otto J. Lehrack (ed.), *No Shining Armor: The Marines at War in Vietnam* (Lawrence: University Press of Kansas, 1992); Kathryn Marshall, *In the Combat Zone: An Oral History of American Women in Vietnam, 1966–1975* (Boston: Little, Brown, 1987); Wallace Terry, *Bloods: An Oral History of the Vietnam War by Black Veterans* (Ballantine, 1984); Philip Caputo, *A Rumor of War* (Ballantine, 1977); and David Donovan, *Once a Warrior King* (McGraw-Hill, 1985). David Maraniss, *They Marched Into*

Sunlight: War and Peace, Vietnam and America, October 1967 (Simon & Schuster, 2003), is an excellent work focusing on two specific events.

Chapter 5

Debate over American failure in Vietnam has been an ongoing and controversial topic. William C. Westmoreland, *A Soldier Reports* (Dell, 1976); and U.S. Grant Sharp, *Strategy for Defeat* (San Rafael, CA: Presidio Press, 1978), are among former military officers who blame civilian restrictions on the armed forces for US defeat. Andrew F. Krepinevich Jr., *The Army and Vietnam* (Baltimore: Johns Hopkins University Press, 1986); and Larry Cable, *Conflict of Myths* (New York University Press, 1986) and *Unholy Grail: The US and the Wars in Vietnam, 1965–8* (London: Routledge, 1991), blame military leadership for fighting a conventional war rather than emphasizing counterinsurgency. Harry G. Summers Jr., *On Strategy* (Novato, CA: Presidio Press, 1982); and Bruce Palmer Jr., *The 25-Year War: America's Military Role in Vietnam* (Lexington: University Press of Kentucky, 1984), argue for more emphasis on conventional strategy, targeting North Vietnam. Both Jeffrey Record, *The Wrong War: Why We Lost in Vietnam* (Annapolis, MD: Naval Institute Press, 1998); and John Prados, *The Hidden History of the Vietnam War* (Chicago: Ivan Dee, 1995), place responsibility for defeat in America's incomprehension of the nature of the war.

Coverage of events after America's departure is available in Arnold R. Isaacs, *Without Honor: Defeat in Vietnam and Cambodia* (Baltimore: Johns Hopkins University Press, 1983); Nguyen Tien Hung and Jerrold Schecter, *The Palace File* (HarperCollins, 1986); Nayan Chanda, *Brother Enemy: The War After the War* (San Diego: Harcourt, Brace, Jovanovich, 1986); James Willbanks, *Abandoning Vietnam: How America Left and South Vietnam Lost its War* (Lawrence: University Press of Kansas, 2004); and P. Edward Haley, *Congress and the Fall of South Vietnam and Cambodia* (Rutherford, NJ: Fairleigh Dickinson University Press, 1982). For the controversial MIA issue, consult H. Bruce Franklin, *M.I.A. or Mythmaking in America* (Brooklyn, NY: Lawrence Hill Books, 1992); and Michael J. Allen, *Until the Last Man Comes Home: POWs, MIAs, and the Unending Vietnam War* (Chapel Hill: University of North Carolina Press, 2009). Christian G. Appy, *American Reckoning: The Vietnam War and Our National Identity* (Viking, 2015), addresses the war's legacy more broadly.

Accounts of the war in Laos include Timothy N. Castle, *At War in the Shadow of Vietnam: U.S. Military Aid to the Royal Lao Government, 1955–1975* (Columbia University Press, 1993); and Jane Hamilton-Merritt, *Tragic Mountains: The Hmong, the Americans, and the Secret Wars for Laos, 1942–1992* (Bloomington: Indiana University Press, 1993). For Cambodia, see Ben Kiernan, *The Pol Pot Regime: Race, Power, and*

Genocide in Cambodia Under the Khmer Rouge, 1975–1979, 2nd edn. (New Haven, CT: Yale University Press, 2002); and David P. Chandler, *The Tragedy of Cambodian History: Politics, War and Revolution since 1945* (New Haven, CT: Yale University Press, 1991).

Memoirs of the South Vietnamese include Bui Diem with David Chanoff, *In the Jaws of History* (Boston: Houghton Mifflin, 1987); Le Ly Hayslip with Jay Wurts, *When Heaven and Earth Changed Places* (Plume, 1989); Nguyen Cao Ky, *Twenty Years and Twenty Days* (Stein and Day, 1976); and Tran Van Don, *Our Endless War: Inside South Vietnam* (San Rafael, CA: Presidio Press, 1978). For personal accounts of the North Vietnamese and NLF, see Van Tien Dung, *Our Great Spring Victory: An Account of the Liberation of South Vietnam* (Monthly Review Press, 1977); Truong Nhu Tang, *A Viet Cong Memoir* (Vintage, 1985); Bui Tin, *Following Ho Chi Minh: Memoirs of a North Vietnamese Colonel* (Honolulu: University of Hawaii Press, 1995); and David Chanoff and Doan Van Toai, *Portrait of the Enemy* (Random House, 1986).

References

Boylan, Kevin M. *Losing Binh Dinh: The Failure of Pacification and Vietnamization, 1969–1971.* Lawrence: University Press of Kansas, 2016.

Braestrup, Peter. *Big Story: How the American Press and Television Reported and Interpreted the Crisis of Tet 1968 in Vietnam and Washington.* Boulder, CO: Westview Press, 1977.

Caputo, Philip. *A Rumor of War.* New York: Ballantine, 1977.

Clarke, Jeffrey J. *Advice and Support: The Final Years, 1965–1973.* Washington, DC: Center of Military History, 1988.

Clifford, Clark. *Counsel to the President.* New York: Random House, 1991.

Cohen, Steven (ed.). *Vietnam: Anthology and Guide to a Television History.* New York: Alfred A. Knopf, 1983.

Congressional Record, 22nd Congress, session 1, pp. 13414–16.

DeBenedetti, Charles, "A CIA Analysis of the Anti-Vietnam War Movement: October 1967", *Peace & Change* 9:1 (Spring 1983): pp. 31–41.

Diem, Bui with David Chanoff. *In the Jaws of History.* Boston, MA: Houghton Mifflin, 1987.

Duiker, William J. *The Communist Road to Power in Vietnam.* Boulder, CO: Westview Press, 1981.

Gibbons, William C. *The U.S. Government and the Vietnam War*, 4 vols. Princeton, NJ: Princeton University Press, 1985–1995.

Graff, Henry. *The Tuesday Cabinet: Deliberation and Decision on Peace and War Under Lyndon B. Johnson.* Englewood Cliffs, NJ: Prentice-Hall, 1970.

Hall, Mitchell K. *Because of Their Faith: CALCAV and Religious Opposition to the Vietnam War.* New York: Columbia University Press, 1990.

Hall, Simon. *Rethinking the American Anti-War Movement.* New York: Routledge, 2012.

Herring, George C. *America's Longest War: The United States and Vietnam, 1950–1975*, 5th edition. New York: McGraw-Hill, 2014.

Hess, Gary R. *The United States' Emergence as a Southeast Asian Power, 1940–1950.* New York: Columbia University Press, 1987.

Ho Chi Minh. *Selected Works*, 4 vols. Hanoi: Foreign Languages Publishing House, 1960–1962.

Isaacs, Arnold R. *Without Honor: Defeat in Vietnam and Cambodia.* Baltimore, MD: John Hopkins University Press, 1983.

Jacobs, Seth. *Cold War Mandarin: Ngo Dinh Diem and the Origins of America's War in Vietnam, 1950–1963.* Lanham, MD: Rowman & Littlefield, 2006.

Johnson, Lyndon Baines. *The Vantage Point: Perspectives of the Presidency, 1963–1969*. New York: Holt, Rinehart and Winston, 1971.

Karnow, Stanley. *Vietnam: A History*. New York: Viking, 1983.

Krepinevich, Andrew F. Jr. *The Army and Vietnam*. Baltimore, MD: Johns Hopkins University Press, 1986.

Logevall, Fredrik. *Embers of War: The Fall of an Empire and the Making of America's Vietnam*. New York: Random House, 2012.

Macdonald, Peter. *Giap: The Victor in Vietnam*. New York: Norton, 1993.

McMahon, Robert J. (ed.) *Major Problems in the History of the Vietnam War*, 3rd edition. Boston, MA: Houghton Mifflin, 2003.

Morris, Roger. *Uncertain Greatness: Henry Kissinger and American Foreign Policy*. New York: Harper & Row, 1977.

Moyar, Mark. *Triumph Forsaken: The Vietnam War, 1954–1965*. Cambridge, UK: Cambridge University Press, 2006.

New York Times, 20 May 1977, p. A17.

Nguyen, Lien-Hang T. *Hanoi's War: An International History of the War for Peace in Vietnam*. Chapel Hill: University of North Carolina Press, 2012.

Nixon, Richard. *RN: The Memoirs of Richard Nixon*. New York: Grossett & Dunlap, 1978.

Oberdorfer, Don. *Tet*. Garden City, NY: Doubleday, 1971.

Oropeza, Lorena. *Raza Si! Guerra No! Chicano Protest and Patriotism During the Viet Nam War Era*. Berkeley: University of California Press, 2005.

Pentagon Papers: The Defense Department History of United States Decision-making on Vietnam, Senator Gravel edition, 5 vols. Boston, MA: Beacon press, 1971–1972.

Public Papers of the Presidents of the United States: Dwight D. Eisenhower 1954. Washington, DC: Government Printing Office, 1958.

Public Papers of the Presidents of the United States: Lyndon B. Johnson, 1963–64. Washington, DC: US Government Printing Office, 1965.

Safire, William. *Before the Fall: An Inside View of the Pre-Watergate White House*. Garden City, NY: Doubleday, 1975.

Schlesinger, Arthur M. Jr. *The Bitter Heritage: Vietnam and American Democracy, 1941–1966*. Boston, MA: Houghton Mifflin, 1966.

Schlight, John (ed.) *The Second Indochina War Symposium*. Washington, DC: US Army Center of Military History, 1986.

Schulzinger, Robert D. *A Time For War: The United States and Vietnam, 1941–1975*. New York: Oxford University Press, 1997.

Sheehan, Neil. *The Pentagon Papers as Published by the New York Times*. New York: Bantam Books, 1971.

Sorley, Lewis. *A Better War: The Unexamined Victories and Final Tragedy of America's Last Years in Vietnam*. San Diego: Harcourt, 1999.

The U.S. Government and the Vietnam War. Executive and Legislative Roles and Relationships. Part IV, July 1965–January 1968. Prepared for the Committee on Foreign Relations, United States Senate by the Congressional Research Service, Library of Congress. Washington, DC: US Government Printing Office, 1994.

Thompson, W. Scott and Donaldson D. Frizzell (ed.) *The Lessons of Vietnam*. New York: Crane & Russak, 1977.

Tucker, Spencer C. (ed.) *Encyclopedia of the Vietnam War: A Political, Social, and Military History*, 3 vols. Santa Barbara, CA: ABC-CLIO, 1998.

Turley, William S. *The Second Indochina War: A Short Political and Military History, 1954–1975*. Boulder, CO: Westview Press, 1986.

U.S. Department of State Bulletin, vol. 22, no. 568, 22 May 1950.

US Department of State Bulletin, vol. 51, no. 1313, 24 August 1964.

US Department of State Bulletin, vol. 52, no. 1343, 22 March 1965.

US Department of State Bulletin, vol. 54, no. 1390, 14 February 1966.

United States Treaties and Other International Agreements, vol. 24, part 1, 1973, pp. 1–224.

United States-Vietnam Relations, 1945–1967: Study Prepared by Department of Defense, printed for the use of House Committee on Armed Services. Book 1, p. A–14. Washington, DC: Government Printing Office, 1971.

Van Dyke, Jon M. *North Vietnam's Strategy for Survival*. Palo Alto, CA: Pacific Books, 1972.

Vietnam: A Television History, "LBJ Goes To War" [video-recording], WGBH Boston Video, 1996.

Weekly Compilation of Presidential Documents, vol. 4, no. 14, 8 April 1968, pp. 619–26.

Weekly Compilation of Presidential Documents, vol. 5, no. 45, 3 November 1969, pp. 1546–55.

Weekly Compilation of Presidential Documents, vol. 6, no. 18, 4 May 1970, pp. 596–601.

Westmoreland, William C. *A Soldier Reports*. New York: Dell, 1976.

Woods, Randall. *LBJ—Architect of American Ambition*. New York: Free Press, 2006.

Zaroulis, Nancy and Gerald Sullivan. *Who Spoke Up? American Protest Against the War in Vietnam, 1963–1975*. Garden City, NY: Doubleday, 1984.

Index